teach® yourself

french phrasebook
ena fowler

For over sixty years, more than
40 million people have learnt over
750 subjects the **teach yourself**
way, with impressive results.

be where you want to be
with **teach yourself**

For UK order enquiries: please contact Bookpoint Ltd, 130 Milton Park, Abingdon, Oxon OX14 4SB. Telephone: +44 (0)1235 827720. Fax: +44 (0)1235 400454. Lines are open 09.00–18.00, Monday to Saturday, with a 24-hour message answering service. Details about our titles and how to order are available at www.teachyourself.co.uk

For USA order enquiries: please contact McGraw-Hill Customer Services, PO Box 545, Blacklick, OH 43004-0545, USA. Telephone: 1-800-722-4726. Fax: 1-614-755-5645.

For Canada order enquiries: please contact McGraw-Hill Ryerson Ltd, 300 Water St, Whitby, Ontario L1N 9B6, Canada. Telephone: 905 430 5000. Fax: 905 430 5020.

Long renowned as the authoritative source for self-guided learning – with more than 30 million copies sold worldwide – the **teach yourself** series includes over 300 titles in the fields of languages, crafts, hobbies, business, computing and education.

British Library Cataloguing in Publication Data: a catalogue record for this title is available from the British Library.

Library of Congress Catalog Card Number: on file.

First published in UK 2004 by Hodder Arnold, 338 Euston Road, London, NW1 3BH.

First published in US 2005 by Contemporary Books, a division of the McGraw-Hill Companies, 1 Prudential Plaza, 130 East Randolph Street, Chicago, IL 60601 USA.

This edition published 2004.

The **teach yourself** name is a registered trade mark of Hodder Headline Ltd.

Author: Ena Fowler

Text and illustrations © Hodder & Stoughton Educational 2004

Printed and bound by Graphycems, Spain.

Impression number 10 9 8 7 6 5 4 3 2 1

Year 2010 2009 2008 2007 2006 2005 2004

CONTENTS

3

INTRODUCTION

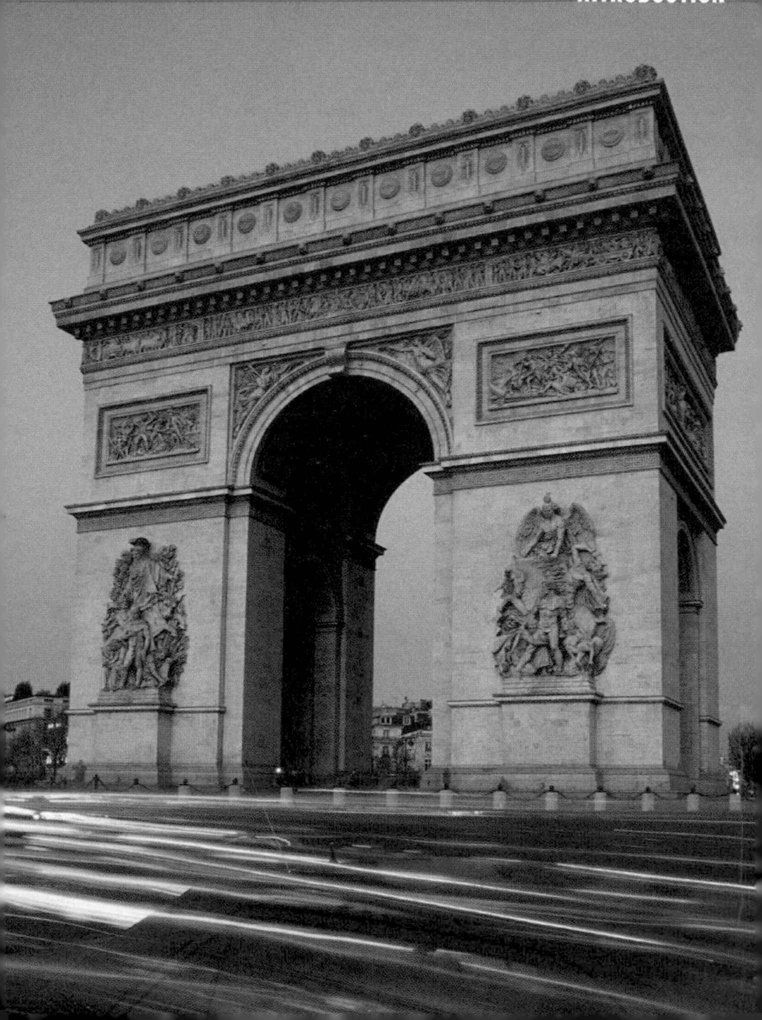

INTRODUCTION

If you know very little French, or need to brush up what you once knew, this *Teach Yourself French Phrasebook* is for you. It covers the situations you are likely to meet on a holiday or short journey abroad.

In addition to the vocabulary, some websites and addresses have been included to provide practical help. The Contents list makes it easy to find the words for the particular situation you are in, while the general vocabulary at the end is handy for reference.

The words in italics below each phrase are a guide to the actual sound of the words, which is sometimes quite different from what we would expect from the spelling. The key to this is on the following page. If you can find a native French speaker to read the key aloud, you will soon get a good idea of the pronunciation.

Don't be discouraged if at first you forget what you thought you had learnt the day before. To learn ten words a day thoroughly is a worthwhile achievement. Before long you will find that through repeated use, the words are becoming unforgettable.

Bon voyage, et bonne chance!

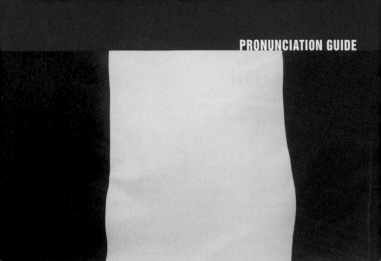

PRONUNCIATION GUIDE

French words do not have very pronounced stresses. If there is a stress, it is normally on the last syllable. The sound **ew**, as in 'tu', is not pronounced like the English 'few', but is more like an **ee** sound spoken with the lips in the position for **oo**. **e-y** is a two-part sound: combine the **e** from 'other' with the **ee** from 'me'.

ay and **oh** are *not* two-part sounds. They are pronounced as short, simple sounds, without the final 'ee' or 'oo' they have in English. French 'r' is always strongly pronounced at the back of the mouth. Therefore '**car**' (= 'because' in French) is not pronounced the same way as the English word 'car', where the 'r' is hardly heard, but as 'ca+r'.

Finally, there are several nasal sounds in French: these are characterised by the presence of an 'n' (η) which is not sounded like the 'n' in English 'can', but more like the 'n' in English 'singing'.

Symbol		French word		English
a	as in	salle	*compare with*	family
ay		marché		faded
e		le		other
ee		il		eel
eh		est		men
eh-y		soleil		very (without the 'r')
er		deux		purr (without the 'r')
err		heure		purr (with the 'r')
ew		tu		see opposite page
e-y		feuille		see opposite page
j		je		pleasure
o		solide		pot
oh		trop		wrote
sh		chien		shoot
s		ici		cereal
k		canard		cook

nasals

ahŋ	sans
aŋ	médecin
oŋ	carton
uŋ	un
yaŋ	bien

USEFUL EVERYDAY PHRASES

yes	oui *wee*
no	non *noŋ*
please	s'il vous plaît *seel voo pleh*
thank you	merci *mehrsee*
sorry	pardon/excusez-moi *pardoŋ/ehxkewzay mwa*
pardon?	pardon? *pardoŋ?*

Hello	Bonjour *boɲjoor*
How are you?	Comment allez-vous? *komahɲt alay voo?*
Goodbye	Au revoir *oh rvwar*
Help!	Au secours! *oh skoor!*
I am ill	Je suis malade *jswee malad*
How much is it?	C'est combien? *seh koɲbyaɲ?*
What does that mean?	Qu'est-ce que ça veut dire? *kehske sa ver deer?*
I don't know	Je ne sais pas *je ne seh pah*
Good morning	Bonjour *boɲjoor*
Good afternoon	Bonjour *boɲjoor*
Good evening	Bonsoir *boɲswar*
Good night	Bonne nuit *bon nwee*
I don't speak French	Je ne parle pas français *je ne parl pah fraɲhseh*
Could you speak more slowly?	Pouvez-vous parler plus lentement? *poovay voo parlay plew lahɲtmahɲ?*
I didn't understand	Je n'ai pas compris *jnay pah koɲpree*

Do you speak English?	Parlez-vous anglais? *parlay vooz ahηgleh?*
Where are the toilets?	Où sont les toilettes s'il vous plaît monsieur/madame/ mademoiselle? *oo soη lay twaleht seel voo pleh msyer/madam/madmwazehl?*
Can you help me?	Pouvez-vous m'aider, s'il vous plaît? *poovay voo mehday seel voo pleh?*
It's	C'est *seh*
It's not	Ce n'est pas *sneh pah*
What is it?	Qu'est-ce que c'est? *kehskeseh?*
good	bon *boη*
bad	mauvais *mohveh*
more	plus *plew*
less	moins *mwaη*
better	mieux *myer*
worse	pire *peer*
too	trop *troh*
where	où *oo*

It is important to add *s'il vous plaît, merci, monsieur, madame* or *mademoiselle* to your enquiries; not to do so seems much ruder in French than in English.

when	quand *kahη*
how	comment *komahη*
must I/we/one...?	faut-il...? *fohteel...?*
can I/we/one...?	peut-on...? *pertohη...?*
will you...?	voulez-vous...? *voolay-voo...?*
I'd like	Je voudrais *je voodreh*
these	ceux-ci *sersee*
those	ceux-là *serla*

Use of *tu* or *vous*: as a general rule, *tu* is used when speaking to relatives, close friends and children.
Teenagers and students use *tu* among themselves.
Vous is used elsewhere. It is not polite to use *tu* to an adult stranger or a shopkeeper.
Merci on its own in reply to a question such as 'Would you like some tea?' means 'No, thank you', so say '*Oui, merci*' if you would like some.

NUMBERS, DAYS, MONTHS, CONVERSIONS, TIME

NUMBERS

1	un *un*		16	seize *sehz*
2	deux *der*		17	dix-sept *deeset*
3	trois *trwa*		18	dix-huit *deezweet*
4	quatre *katr*		19	dix-neuf *deeznerf*
5	cinq *sank*		20	vingt *van*
6	six *sees*		21	vingt et un *vant ay un*
7	sept *set*		22	vingt-deux *van der*
8	huit *weet*		23	vingt-trois *van trwa*
9	neuf *nerf*		24	vingt-quatre *van katr*
10	dix *dees*		25	vingt-cinq *van sank*
11	onze *onz*		26	vingt-six *van sees*
12	douze *dooz*		27	vingt-sept *van set*
13	treize *trehz*		28	vingt-huit *vant weet*
14	quatorze *katorz*		29	vingt-neuf *van nerf*
15	quinze *kanz*		30	trente *trahnt*

40	quarante *karahnt*	80	quatre-vingts *katr van*
50	cinquante *sankahnt*	90	quatre-vingt-dix *katr van dees*
60	soixante *swasahnt*	100	cent *sahn*
70	soixante-dix *swasahnt dees*	200	deux cents *der sahn*

DAYS OF THE WEEK

Sunday	dimanche *deemahnsh*	Thursday	jeudi *jerdee*
Monday	lundi *lundee*	Friday	vendredi *vahndredee*
Tuesday	mardi *mardee*	Saturday	samedi *samdee*
Wednesday	mercredi *mehrkredee*		

MONTHS

January	janvier *jahnvyay*	July	juillet *jweeyeh*
February	février *fayvreeay*	August	août *oot*
March	mars *mars*	September	septembre *sehptahnbr*
April	avril *avreel*	October	octobre *oktobr*
May	mai *meh*	November	novembre *novahnbr*
June	juin *jwan*	December	décembre *daysahnbr*

Note: 'The 3rd of June' is expressed as 'the three June', i.e. *le trois juin*. The other dates are similarly expressed, except for the first of the month, which is *le premier*, not *le un*.

You can obtain a free brochure giving advice about driving abroad by phoning the AA or RAC (whether you are a member or not) – see page 74.

TEMPERATURE

°F	0	20	32	50	70	87	98.6	105	212
°C	–18	–3	0	10	21	30	36.9	40	100

LIQUIDS

litres	5	10	15	20	25
imperial gallons	1.1	2.2	3.3	4.4	5.5
US gallons	1.3	2.6	3.9	5.2	6.5

litres	30	35	40	45	50
imperial gallons	6.6	7.7	8.8	9.9	11.0
US gallons	7.8	9.1	10.4	11.7	13.0

WEIGHTS

e.g. 1 kg = 2.2 lb, 1 lb = 0.46 kg

kg	1/2	1	2	3	4	5
lb	1.1	2.2	4.4	6.6	8.8	11.0

lb	1	2	3	4	5
kg	0.45	0.90	1.36	1.81	2.27

lb	6	7	8	9	10
kg	2.76	3.22	3.68	4.14	4.6

NB 1000 g = 1 kg

TIME

1 **'Quarters and halves'.** Say Table 1 out loud. You can make 39 sentences from this. Translate as you go. By the time you've finished, you'll know how to tell the time!
  E.g. '*Il est une heure et quart.*' 'It's quarter past one.'
  '*Il est une heure et demie.*' 'It's half past one.'

Table 1

	one	une	*ewn*	moins le quart
	two	deux	*derz*	*mwan le kar*
	three	trois	*trwaz*	(quarter to)
It is	four	quatre	*katr*	
(It's)	five	cinq	*sank*	
Il est	six	six	*seez*	heure(s) et quart
eel eh	seven	sept	*seht*	*err* *ay kar*
	eight	huit	*weet*	(quarter past)
	nine	neuf	*nerv*	
	ten	dix	*deez*	et demi(e)
	eleven	onze	*onz*	*ay dmee*
				(half past)
	noon	midi	*meedee*	
	midnight	minuit	*meenwee*	

---

2 'Fives and tens'. Do the same for Table 2.

E.g. '*Il est une heure cinq.*' 'It's five past one.'
'*Il est neuf heures moins cinq.*' 'It's five to nine.'

Table 2

	one	une	*ewn*	
	two	deux	*derz*	cinq (five past)
	three	trois	*trwaz*	dix (10 past)
It is	four	quatre	*katr*	vingt (20 past)
(It's)	five	cinq	*sank*	vingt-cinq (25 past)
Il est	six	six	*seez*	heure(s) moins vingt-cinq
eel eh	seven	sept	*seht*	*err* (25 to)
	eight	huit	*weet*	moins vingt (20 to)
	nine	neuf	*nerv*	moins dix (10 to)
	ten	dix	*deez*	moins cinq (5 to)
	eleven	onze	*onz*	*mwan sank (etc.)*

The 24-hour clock. For this you need to know the numbers from 13 to 59.

Table 3

1 pm		treize	13 *trehz*
2 pm		quatorze	14 *katorz*
3 pm		quinze	15 *kaŋz*
4 pm		seize	16 *sehz*
5 pm		dix-sept	17 *deeseht*
6 pm	Il est *(eel eh)*	dix-huit	18 *deezweet*
7 pm		dix-neuf	19 *deeznerv*
8 pm		vingt	20 *vaŋt*
9 pm		vingt et une	21 *vaŋt ay ewn*
10 pm		vingt-deux	22 *van derz*
11 pm		vingt-trois	23 *van trwaz*
12 pm		vingt-quatre	24 *van katr*

heures *(err)*

To add the minutes, use Table 1, except for the 'quarters and halves'. Instead of *et quart/et demi(e)/moins le quart*, use the numbers 15 *(quinze)*, 30 *(trente)* or 45 *(quarante-cinq)*.

E.g.

treize heures dix	1.10 pm
treize heures trente	1.30 pm
treize heures quarante-cinq	1.45 pm

13h.	Il est treize heures	It's 1 pm
14h.	Il est quatorze heures	It's 2 pm
15h.	Il est quinze heures	It's 3 pm
16h.	Il est seize heures	It's 4 pm
17h.	Il est dix-scpt heures	It's 5 pm
18h.	Il est dix-huit heures	It's 6 pm
19h.	Il est dix-neuf heures	It's 7 pm
20h.	Il est vingt heures	It's 8 pm

21h.	Il est vingt et une heures	It's 9 pm
22h.	Il est vingt-deux heures	It's 10 pm
23h.	Il est vingt-trois heures	It's 11 pm
24h.	Il est vingt-quatre heures	It's 12 midnight

ARRIVAL

Excuse me, where is…?	Excusez-moi, où est…? *ehxkewzay mwa, oo eh…?*
…the car hire	…l'agence de location de voitures *lajahŋs de lokasyoŋ de vwatewr*
…the car park	…le parking *le parkeeng*
…the exchange bureau	…le bureau de change *le bewroh de shahŋj*
…the exit	…la sortie *la sortee*
…the information bureau	…le syndicat d'initiative *le saŋdeeka deeneesyateev*

...the information bureau	...le bureau de renseignements *le bewroh de rahηsehnyemahη*
...the left-luggage office (baggage check)	...la consigne *la koηseenye*
...the Metro	...le Métro *le maytroh*
...the waiting room	...la salle d'attente *la sal datahηt*
...the ticket office	...le guichet *le geesheh*
...the bus stop	...l'arrêt d'autobus *lareh dohtobews*
Excuse me, where are the...?	Excusez-moi, où sont les...? *ehxkewzay mwa, oo soη lay...?*
...taxis	...taxis *taxee*
...toilets	...toilettes *twaleht*
Where can I...?	Où est-ce que je peux...? *oo ehske je per...?*
...find my luggage	...trouver mes bagages *troovay may bagaj*
...get a taxi	...prendre un taxi *prahηdr uh taxee*
How do I get to...?	Pour aller à...? *poor alay a...?*
How far away is the...?	Le/la...est à quelle distance? *le/la...ehta kel deestahηs?*
Is there a bus stop near here?	Y a-t-il un arrêt d'autobus près d'ici? *yateel uη areh dohtobews preh deesee?*

Is it far/near?	Est-ce loin/près? *ehs lwañ/preh?*
Where's the nearest...?	Où est le/la...le/la plus proche? *oo eh le/la...le/la plew prosh?*
Could you repeat that, please?	Voulez-vous répéter, s'il vous plaît? *voolay voo raypaytay, seel voo pleh?*
Could you speak more slowly?	Voulez-vous parler plus lentement? *voolay voo parlay plew lahñtmahñ?*
I didn't understand	Je n'ai pas compris *jnay pah koñpree*

YOU MAY HEAR:

Prenez... *Prenay...*	Take...
...la première rue *la premyehr rew*	...the first street
...la deuxième rue *la derzyehm rew*	...the second street
...à droite/à gauche *a drwat/a gohsh*	...on the right/on the left
Allez tout droit *alay too drwa*	Go straight on
Il faut... *eel foh...*	You have to...
...tourner à droite/à gauche *toornay a drwat/a gohsh*	...turn right/left
au bout de la rue *oh boo de la rew*	at the end of the street

| Il/elle est à deux kilomètres, à peu près
eel/ehl eht a der keelohmetr, a per preh | It's about two kilometres away |

GETTING A TAXI

Where can I get a taxi?	Où est-ce que je peux trouver un taxi? *oo ehske je per troovay un taxee?*
I want to go to...	Je veux aller à... *je ver alay a...*
...this address	...cette adresse *seht adrehs*
...the airport	...l'aéroport *la-ayropor*
...the (bus) station	...la gare (routière) *la gar (rootyehr)*
Not so fast, please!	Moins vite, s'il vous plaît! *mwan veet, seel voo pleh!*
Stop here, please	Arrêtez-vous ici, s'il vous plaît *arehtay voo eesee, seel voo pleh*
Will you wait for me, please?	Voulez-vous m'attendre, s'il vous plaît? *voolay voo matahndr, seel voo pleh?*
How much is it?	C'est combien? *seh konbyan?*
Here's something for you (a tip)	Voici pour vous *vwasee poor voo*
I'm in a hurry	Je suis pressé(e) *jswee prehsay*
Could you help me with my luggage?	Pouvez-vouz m'aider à porter mes bagages? *poovay voo mehday a portay may bagaj?*

HOTELS

If you are without accommodation on arrival in a strange town, you will find a list at the local information office (*Syndicat d'Initiative*). The hotels are given star ratings according to their amenities. You should ask whether or not breakfast and showers are included in the price.

Cheaper (but charming, clean and comfortable) accommodation is often available at *pensions* (boarding houses), *auberges* and *logis de France*. Don't comfuse *auberges* (country inns) with *auberges de jeunesse* (youth hostels).

Loisirs acceuil are officially-backed booking services which reserve hotels, gîtes and campsites, usually free of charge. For a list, send a s.a.e. to Maison de la France, 178 Piccadilly, London W1J 9AL.

When you register at a hotel, boarding house or campsite, you will be asked to fill in a registration form *(une fiche)* and to hand over your passport, which will be returned to you after the details have been taken.

YOU MAY SEE:

Nom/Prénom	**Surname/First name**
Lieu de domicile/rue/n°	**Address/Street/No**
Date/lieu de naissance	**Date/place of birth**
Numéro de passeport	**Passport number**
Lieu/Date	**Place/Date**
Signature	**Signature**

Is there a hotel near here?	Est-ce qu'il y a un hôtel près d'ici? *ehskeelya un ohtehl preh deesee?*
My name is...	Je m'appelle... *jmapehl...*
I have a reservation	J'ai réservé *jay rayzehrvay*
We're staying for one night	On va rester une nuit *on va restay ewn nwee*
There are two of us	Nous sommes deux *noo som der*

AT A HOTEL

Have you any rooms?	Avez-vous des chambres? *avay voo day shahmbr?*
No, I haven't booked	Non, je n'ai pas réservé *noη, jnay pah raysehrvay*
I'd like to book a room	Je voudrais réserver une chambre *je voodreh rayservay ewn shahηbr*

What is the cost of a room...?	Quel est le prix d'une chambre...?
	kehl eh le pree dewn shahηbr...?
...for one	...pour une personne
	poor ewn pehrson
...for two	...pour deux personnes
	poor der pehrson
...for a family	...de famille
	de famee
...with one bed	...avec un lit
	avehk uη lee
...with a double bed	...avec grand lit
	avehk graη lee
...with two beds	...avec deux lits
	avehk der lee
...with an extra bed	...avec lit supplémentaire
	avehk lee sewplaymahηtehr
...with a shower	...avec douche
	avehk doosh
...without a shower	...sans douche
	sahη doosh
...with a bathroom	...avec salle de bains
	avehk sal de baη
...without a bathroom	...sans salle de bains
	sahη sal de baη
...with a toilet	...avec WC
	avehk vay say
Our party consists of two adults and three children	Nous sommes deux adultes et trois enfants
	noo som derz adewlt ay trwaz ahηfahη
How much is it...?	C'est combien...?
	seh koηbyaη...?
...per day	...par jour
	par joor

...per person
...par personne
par pehrson

...per night
...par nuit
par nwee

...weekly
...par semaine
par smehn

...for half-board
...la demi-pension
la dmee pahŋsyoŋ

...for full board
...la pension complète
la pahŋsyoŋ koŋpleht

Is breakfast included?
Le petit déjeuner est compris?
le ptee dayjernay eh koŋpree?

Are tax and service included?
Taxes et service compris?
tax ay sehrvees koŋpree?

Is there a reduced rate for children?
Y a-t-il un tarif réduit pour les enfants?
yateel uŋ tareef raydwee poor layz ahŋfahŋ?

What floor is the room on?
La chambre est à quel étage?
la shahŋbr ehta kehluytuj?

On the ground floor
Au rez-de-chaussée
oh ray de shohsay

On the second floor
Au deuxième étage
oh derzyehm aytaj

On the third floor
Au troisième étage
oh trwazyehm aytaj

On the fourth floor
Au quatrième étage
oh katryehm aytaj

Is there a lift?
Y a-t-il un ascenseur?
yateel uŋ assahŋserr?

It's too expensive
C'est trop cher
seh troh shehr

Have you anything cheaper?	Avez-vous quelque chose de moins cher? *avay voo kehlkeshohz de mwan shehr?*
We'll take them, please	On les prend, s'il vous plaît *on lay prahn, seel voo pleh*
We are leaving on Sunday	On part dimanche *on par deemahnsh*
Do you want a deposit?	Voulez-vous une caution? *voolay voo ewn kohsyon?*
Do you want to see our passports?	Voulez-vous voir nos passeports? *voolay voo vwar noh paspor?*
At what time can we...?	A quelle heure est-ce qu'on...? *a kehl err ehskon...?*
...have breakfast	...prend le petit déjeuner *prahn le ptee dayjernay*
...have lunch	...déjeune *dayjern*
...dine	...dîne *deen*
How far away is...?	...est à quelle distance? *ehta kehl deestahns?*
...the beach	La plage... *la plaj...*
...the railway station	La gare... *la gar...*
...the centre of town	Le centre-ville... *le sahntrveel...*
May I have...	Voulez-vous me donner... *voolay voo me donay*
...the bill	...la note *la not*

...a key
...une clef
ewn klay

...an extra pillow
...un oreiller supplémentaire
uη orehyay sewplaymahηtehr

...some soap
...du savon
dew savoη

...a towel
...une serviette
ewn sehrvyeht

...an ashtray
...un cendrier
uη sahηdreeay

...an extra blanket
...une couverture supplémentaire
ewn koovehrtewr sewplaymahηtehr

...some writing paper
...du papier à lettres
dew papyay a lehtr

...some toilet paper
...du papier hygiénique
dew papyay eejeeayneek

I haven't got one/any
Je n'en ai pas
jnahη ay pah

basement
le sous-sol
le soo sol

deposit
la caution
la kohsyoη

form
la fiche
la feesh

ground floor
le rez-de-chaussée
le ray de shohsay

lift (elevator)
un ascenseur
uη assahηserr

luggage
les bagages
lay bagaj

to pay the bill
régler la note
rayglay la not

payment	le règlement
	le rehglmahη
staircase	un escalier
	uη ehskalyay
telephone	le téléphone
	le taylayfon
washbasin	le lavabo
	le lavaboh
bathroom	la salle de bains
	la sal de baη
light bulb	une ampoule
	ewn aηpool
maid	la femme de chambre
	la fam de shahηbr
safe	le coffre-fort
	le koffr for
garage	le garage
	le garaj
manager	le propriétaire
	le propreeaytehr

YOU MAY HEAR:

Vous avez réservé?	Have you booked?
vooz avay raysehrvay?	
Vous avez des pièces d'identité?	Have you any identification?
vooz avay day pyehs deedahηteetay?	
Les repas ne sont pas compris	Meals are not included
lay repah ne soη pah koηpree	
Il n'y a pas d'ascenseur	There isn't a lift
eel nya pah dassahηserr	
Voulez-vous remplir cette fiche?	Would you fill in this form?
voolay voo rahηpleer set feesh?	

Signez ici, s'il vous plaît
seenyay eesee seel voo pleh

Sign here, please

Vous restez combien de nuits?
voo restay koηbyaη de nwee?

How long are you staying?

Il n'y a pas de place
eel nya pah de plas

There is no room

**Could you bring breakfast to
my room?**

Pouvez-vous m'apporter le petit
déjeuner dans ma chambre?
*poovay voo maportay le ptee
dayjernay daη ma shahηbr?*

Could you call me at 7 o'clock?

Pouvez-vous m'appeler à
sept heures?
poovay voo maplay a set err?

Do you have foreign newspapers?

Avez-vous des journaux
étrangers?
*avay voo day joornoh
aytrahηjay?*

CHECKING OUT

May I have the bill please?

L'addition, s'il vous plaît
ladisyoη seel voo pleh

Is everything included?

Tout est compris?
toot eh koηpree?

Can I pay by credit card?

Puis-je payer avec une
carte de crédit?
*pweej payay avehk ewn
kart de kraydee?*

Can you get us a taxi?

Pouvez-vous nous appeler
un taxi?
poovay voo nooz aplay uη taxee?

**Could somebody bring down
our luggage?**

Est-ce que quelqu'un pourrait
descendre nos bagages?
*ehske kehlkuη pooreh daysahηdr
noh bagaj?*

Here's the forwarding address	Faites suivre le courrier à cette adresse *feht sweevr le kooryay a seht adrehs*
Could we have our passports, please?	Pourriez-vous nous rendre nos passeports? *pooryay voo noo rahηdr no passpor?*
I must leave immediately	Il faut que je parte tout de suite *eel foh ke je part toot sweet*
How much were the telephone calls?	À combien se monte ma note de téléphone? *a koηbyaη se moηt ma not de taylayfon?*
I think there's a mistake on the bill	Je crois qu'il y a erreur sur la note *je krwa keelya ehrer sewr la not*
You've charged too much	Vous m'avez trop compté sur la note *voo mavay troh koηtay sewr la not*

CAMPING / CARAVANNING

Camping in France provides a comparatively inexpensive way
to see the country, and the sites are usually very well
organised. Off-site camping is not always allowed (look out for
camping interdit 'forbidden' signs).
Official campsites have a star rating, according to amenities.
You usually have to pay separately for the plot, the vehicle,
electricity and showers.
When youth hostelling, you will be asked for your YHA card
and passport when you arrive.

Electricity
In most areas, this is the same voltage as Britain (220V), but
the power points are different, and you need a special adaptor
(available in Britain).

Where is the the nearest campsite?	Où se trouve le camping le plus proche? *oo se troov le kahηpeeng le plew prosh?*
Is it expensive?	C'est cher? *seh shehr?*

CAMPING

I'd like to hire...	Je voudrais louer... *je voodreh looay...*
Have you...?	Avez-vous...? *avay voo...?*
How much does...cost?	C'est combien pour...? *seh koηbyaη poor...?*
I have booked	J'ai réservé *jay rayzehrvay*
I haven't booked	Je n'ai pas réservé *jnay pah rayzehrvay*

Lists of campsites and youth hostels can be obtained from Maison de la
France, 178 Piccadilly, London W1V 9AL, and at the main railway stations.

a bed	un lit *uη lee*
a blanket	une couverture *ewn koovehrtewr*
a car	une voiture *ewn vwatewr*
a caravan	une caravane *ewn karavan*
electricity	l'électricité *laylehktreeseetay*
one person	une personne *ewn pehrson*
sheets	des draps *day dra*
a shower	une douche *ewn doosh*
a sleeping bag	un sac de couchage *uη sak de kooshaj*
a site	un emplacement *uη ahηplasmahη*
a tent	une tente *ewn tahnt*
youth hostel	une auberge de jeunesse *ewen ohbehrj de jernehs*
for one night	pour une nuit *poor ewn nwee*
for two nights	pour deux nuits *poor der nwee*
for a week	pour une semaine *poor ewn smehn*
Where is/are...?	Où est/sont...? *oo eh/soη...?*

...the bar	...le bar *le bar*
...the dormitory	...le dortoir *le dortwar*
...the car park	...le parking *le parkeeng*
...the food store	...l'alimentation *laleemahηtasyoη*
...the launderette	...la laverie *la lavree*
...the pancake parlour	...la crêperie *la krehpree*
...the reception office	...le bureau d'accueil *le bewroh dak-e-y*
...the restaurant	...le restaurant *le rehstohrahη*
...the self-service	...le libre-service *le leebr sehrvees*
...the snack bar	...le snack *le snak*
...the showers	...les douches *lay doosh*
...the toilets	...les toilettes *lay twaleht*
Can you lend me...	Pouvez-vous me prêter... *poovay voo me prehtay...*
...a corkscrew	...un tire-bouchon *uη teer booshoη*
...a frying pan	...une poêle *ewn pwal*
...a knife	...un couteau *uη kootoh*

...some matches	...des allumettes *dayz alewmeht*
...a saucepan	...une casserole *ewn kassrol*
...a spoon	...une cuillère *ewn kweeyehr*
...a tin opener	...un ouvre-boîte *uη oovr bwat*
There isn't any hot water	Il n'y a pas d'eau chaude *eel nya pah doh shohd*
There aren't any matches	Il n'y a pas d'allumettes *eel nya pah dalewmeht*
The light isn't working	La lumière ne fonctionne pas *la lewmyehr ne foηksyon pah*
the plug/socket	la prise *la preez*
the tap	le robinet *le robeenay*
The toilet is blocked	Le WC est bouché *le vaysay eh booshay*
The window is jammed	La fenêtre est coincée *la fenehtr eh kwaηsay*

EATING OUT

Some meals, as well as the usual coffee and drinks, are obtainable at bars, bistros, snack bars and cafés. Prices are often more expensive at the tables than at the bar, and even more expensive outside on the verandah.

Salons de thé specialise in pastries, ice cream and tea or coffee. Meals are occasionally served.

Full meals are found in railway station buffets (often surprisingly good), *brasseries*, *routiers*, *restoroutes* and *auberges*. The most expensive meals are served in *hostelleries*, *relais de campagne*, *rôtisseries* and *restaurants*.

Lunch *(le déjeuner)* is served between 12 and 2 pm. The evening meal *(le dîner)* is normally served between 8 and 10 pm.

In restaurants you will be able to choose between the fixed-price menu with several courses *(le menu)* and the *à la carte menu*, where you may have as few or as many courses as you like.

I'm hungry	J'ai faim *jay faη*
I'm thirsty	J'ai soif *jay swaf*
Can you recommend a good restaurant?	Pouvez-vous recommander un bon restaurant? *poovay voo rekomahηday uη boh restorahη?*
Are there any inexpensive restaurants around here?	Y a-t-il des restaurants pas très chers près d'ici? *yateel day restorahη pah treh shehr preh deesee?*
I'd like to reserve a table for four	Je voudrais réserver une table pour quatre personnes *je voodreh rayservay ewn tabl poor katr pehrson*
for 8 o'clock	à huit heures *a weet err*
Could we have a table...	Pourriez-vous nous mettre *pooryay voo noo mehtr...*
...in the corner	...dans le coin *dahη le kwaη*
...by the window	...à côté de la fenêtre *a kohtay de la fenehtr*
...outside	...sur la terrasse *sewr la terras*

...in a non-smoking area	...dans un endroit pour les non-fumeurs *dahηzun ahηdrwa poor lay noη fewmerr*
Give me...	Donnez-moi... *donay mwa*
I'd like...	Je voudrais... *je voodreh*
We'd like...	Nous voudrions... *noo voodreeoη*
...a beer	...une bière *ewn byehr*
...two white coffees	...deux crèmes *der krehm*
	...deux cafés au lait *der kafay oh leh*
...one black coffee	...un café nature *uη kafay natewr*
	...un café noir *uη kafay nwar*
...an espresso	...un café express *uη kafay esprehs*
...a fruit juice	... un jus de fruits *uη jew de frwee*
...a hamburger	...un hamburger *uη ahηbewgerr*
...a toasted cheese and ham sandwich	...un croque-monsieur *uη krok msyer*
...one/two pancakes	...une crêpe/deux crêpes *ewn krehp/der krehp*
...some chips	...des frites *day freet*

What sort of sandwich do you have?	Qu'est-ce que vous avez comme sandwiches? *kehske vooz avay kom sandveesh?*
I'll have a ...sandwich	Je prends un sandwich au... *je prahn un sahndveesh oh...*
...cheese	...fromage *fromaj*
...ham	...jambon *jahnbon*
...pâté	...pâté *pahtay*
...sausage	...salami *salamee*

YOU MAY HEAR:

Vous avez choisi? *vooz avay shwazee?*	Have you chosen?
Et pour suivre? *ay poor sweevr?*	Anything to follow?
C'est tout? *seh too?*	Is that all?
Je vous recommande ceci *je voo rekomahnd sesee*	I recommend this
Qu'est-ce que vous allez boire? *kehske voozalay bwar?*	What would you like to drink?
Nous n'avons pas de... *noo navon pah de...*	We don't have any...

YOU MAY SEE:

Menu à prix fixe	Set menu
Garniture au choix	Choice of accompanying vegetables

Supplément	Extra charge
Pour deux personnes	For two people

ORDERING A MEAL

Is there a table available please?	Y a-t-il une table de libre, s'il vous plaît? *yateel ewn tabl de leebr, seel voo pleh?*
There are two/three/four of us	Nous sommes deux/trois/quatre *noo som der/trwa/katr*
Will you bring me...?	Voudriez-vous m'apporter...? *voodreeay voo maportay...?*
...the set menu	...le menu à prix fixe *le menew a pree feex*
...the à la carte menu	...la carte *la kart*
...the 25-euro menu	...le menu à vingt-cinq euros *le menew a van sank erroh*
...today's special menu	...le menu du jour *le menew dew joor*
I'll have...	Je prends... *je prahn*
...the cold meat	...la charcuterie *la sharkewtree*
...the salad	...la salade/les crudités *la salad/luy krewdeetay*
...today's special	...le plat du jour *le pla dew joor*
Waiter!	Monsieur! *msyer!*
Waitress!	Mademoiselle! *mamwazehl!*

Excuse me, I haven't got a...	Excusez-moi, je n'ai pas de...
	ehxkewzay mwa, jnay pah de...
...ashtray	...cendrier
	sahŋdreeay
...cup	...tasse
	tas
...fork	...fourchette
	foorsheht
...glass	...verre
	vehr
...knife	...couteau
	kootoh
...plate	...assiette
	asyeht
...saucer	...soucoupe
	sookoop
...spoon	...cuillère
	kweeyehr
cover charge	le couvert
	le koovehr
Do you have any vegetarian dishes?	Avez-vous des plats végétariens?
	avay voo day pla vayjaytaryaŋ?
that's enough	ça suffit
	sa sewfee
tipping not allowed	pourboire interdit
	poorbwar aŋtehrdee
Just a small portion	Juste une petite portion
	jewst ewn pteet porsyoŋ
Can I have more...	Un peu plus de..., s'il vous plaît
	uŋ per plew de...seel voo pleh
It's...	C'est...
	seh...

...delicious	...délicieux *dayleesyer*
...burnt	...brûlé *brewlay*
...just right	...à point *a pwaη*
...overcooked	...trop cuit *troh kwee*
...well done	...bien cuit *byaη kwee*
...too salty	...trop salé *troh salay*
...too sweet	...trop sucré *troh sewkray*

YOU MAY HEAR:

Suivez-moi, s'il vous plaît *sweevay mwa, seel voo pleh*	Follow me, please
Vous avez choisi? *vooz avay shwazee?*	Have you chosen?
Que voulez-vous pour commencer? *ke voolay voo poor komaηsay?*	What would you like to start?
Et pour suivre? *ay poor sweevr?*	And to follow?
Et comme boisson? *ay kom bwasoη?*	And what would you like to drink?
Bon appétit! *bonapaytee!*	Enjoy your meal!

PAYING

Waiter! Will you bring the bill, please?	Monsieur! Voulez-vous apporter l'addition, s'il vous plaît? *msyer! voolay voo aportay ladeesyon, seel voo pleh?*
Is service included?	Est-ce que le service est compris? *ehske le sehrvees eh konpree?*
Is the cover charge included?	Est-ce que le couvert est compris? *ehske le koovehr eh konpree?*
Do you accept traveller's cheques?	Est-ce que vous acceptez les chèques de voyage? *ehske vooz aksehptay lay shehk de vwayaj?*
Do you accept credit cards?	Est-ce que vous acceptez les cartes de crédit? *ehske vooz aksehptay lay kart de kraydee?*
Have you got change?	Avez-vous de la monnaie? *avay voo de la moneh?*
Keep the change	Gardez la monnaie *garday la moneh*
This is for you	Voici pour vous *vwasee poor voo*
Excuse me, there's been a mistake	Excusez-moi, il y a erreur *ehxkewzay mwa, eelya ehrerr*
I/we had...	On a pris... *on a pree...*
...the fixed-price meal	...le menu à prix fixe *le menew a pree feex*
...a bottle of...	...une bouteille de... *ewn booteh-y de...*
...the roast beef	...le rosbif *le rosbeef*

How much is that?	C'est combien, ça? *seh koɳbyaɳ,sa?*
But you have put... euros on the bill	Mais vous avez mis...euros sur l'addition *meh vooz avay mee...erroh sewr laddeesyoɳ*
I/we ordered...	On a commandé... *oɳ a komahɳday...*
But I/we didn't order...	Mais on n'a pas commandé... *meh oɳ na pah komahɳday...*
You have put it on the bill	Vous l'avez mis sur l'addition *voo lavay mee sewr ladeesyoɳ*
You are wrong	Vous avez tort *vooz avay tor*
You are right	Vouz avez raison *vooz avay rehzoɳ*

YOU MAY HEAR:

Le service est compris *le sehrvees eh koɳpree*	Service is included
Voulez-vous du café? *voolay voo dew kaffay?*	Would you like a coffee?
Voulez-vous un dessert? *voolay voo un daysehr?*	Would you like a dessert?
Il n'y en a pas *eel nyahɳ a pah*	We don't have any
Je vais le changer tout de suite *je veh le shahɳjay toot sweet*	I'll change it right away

MENU GUIDE

UNDERSTANDING THE MENU

HORS D'OEUVRES

assiette anglaise
asyeht ahŋglehz

assiette de charcuterie
asyeht de sharkewtree

crudités
krewdeetay

hors d'oeuvre variés
or dervr vareeeay

jambon
jahŋboŋ

oeufs
er

pâté
pahtay

salade mêlangée
salad mehlahŋjay

saucisson
sohseesoŋ

SOUPES

bouillon/consommé
booyon/koŋsomay

crème/velouté
krehm/vlootay

potage
potaj

pot-au-feu
pot oh fer

STARTERS

assorted cold roast meats

assorted cold (pork) meats

salad or raw vegetables

assorted hors d'oeuvres

ham

eggs

pâté

mixed salad

sausage

SOUPS

clear soup

cream soup

thick soup

thick vegetable soup with meat

soupe du jour *soop dew joor*	soup of the day
soupe à l'oignon *soop a lonyon*	French onion soup

OMELETTES

OMELETTES

omelette nature *omleht natewr*	plain omelette
omelette aux champignons *omleht oh shahnpeenyon*	mushroom omelette
omelette au jambon *omleht oh jahnbon*	ham omelette

POISSONS

FISH DISHES

anchois *ahnshwa*	anchovies
cabillaud/morue *kabeeyoh/morew*	cod
carrelet *karelay*	plaice
crevettes *kreveht*	shrimps
écrevisses *aykrevees*	crayfish
harengs *arahn*	herring
homard *omar*	lobster
huîtres *weetr*	oysters
langoustines/scampi *lahngoosteen/scahnpee*	prawns/scampi
moules *mool*	mussels

saumon *sohmon*	salmon
thon *ton*	tuna
truite *trweet*	trout

VIANDE

MEAT AND POULTRY DISHES

agneau *anyoh*	lamb
bifteck *beeftehk*	steak
saignant *sehnyan*	rare
à point *a pwan*	medium
bien cuit *byan kwee*	well done
boeuf *berf*	beef
charcuterie *sharkewtree*	pork products
côte *koht*	rib
côtelette *kohtleht*	chop
dinde *dand*	turkey
filet *feelay*	fillet
lapin *lapan*	rabbit

lard *lar*	bacon
poulet *pooleh*	chicken
rosbif *rosbeef*	roast beef
porc *por*	pork
veau *voh*	veal
volaille *vola-y*	poultry

LÉGUMES, RIZ ET PÂTES
VEGETABLES, RICE AND PASTA

asperges *aspehrj*	asparagus
betterave *behtrahv*	beetroot
carottes *karot*	carrots
champignons *shaηpeenyoη*	mushrooms
choucroûte *shookroot*	sauerkraut
chou-fleur *shooflerr*	cauliflower
épinards *aypeenar*	spinach
haricots blancs *areekoh blahη*	haricot beans
haricots verts *areekoh vehr*	green beans

maïs *maees*	sweetcorn
nouilles *nooye*	noodles
pâtes *paht*	pasta
petits pois *ptee pwah*	peas
oignons *onyoη*	onions
pommes de terre *pom de tehr*	potatoes
duchesse/mousseline *dewshehs/moosleen*	mashed
nature/vapeur *natewr/vaperr*	boiled/steamed
pommes frites *pom freet*	chips
riz *ree*	rice
salade *salad*	lettuce

DESSERTS

DESSERTS

fraises à la crème *frehz ala krehm*	strawberries and cream
framboises à la crème *frahηbwaz ala krehm*	raspberries and cream
glace à la vanille *glas ala vaneeye*	vanilla ice-cream
glace au citron *glas oh seetroη*	lemon ice-cream

pâtisseries *pahteesree*	cakes
pêche melba *pehsh mehlba*	peaches with ice-cream
tarte aux pommes *tart oh pom*	apple tart
...aux cerises *oh sreez*	cherry tart
...aux fraises *oh frehz*	strawberry tart
yaourt *yaoort*	yoghurt

FRUITS ET FROMAGES — FRUIT AND CHEESE

ananas *anana*	pineapple
bananes *banan*	bananas
fraises *frehz*	strawberries
framboises *frahŋbwaz*	raspberries
fromage *fromaj*	cheese
oranges *orahŋj*	oranges
pamplemousse *pahŋplemoos*	grapefruit
poires *pwar*	pears
pommes *pom*	apples

prunes *prewn*	plums
abricots *abreekoh*	apricots
brugnons *brewnyoη*	nectarines
cassis *kasees*	blackcurrant
cerises *sereez*	cherries
citron *seetroη*	lemon
pêches *pehsh*	peaches
raisins *rehzaη*	grapes

BOISSONS

DRINKS

J'aimerais ... de *jehmereh...de*	I'd like a ... of
...une bouteille *ewn booteh-y*	...bottle
...une demi-bouteille *ewn dmee booteh-y*	...half bottle
...une carafe *ewn karaf*	...carafe
...un verre *uη vehr*	...glass
vin rouge *vaη rooj*	red wine
vin blanc *vaη blahη*	white wine

rosé
rohzay

rosé

sec
sehk

dry

doux
doo

sweet

mousseux
mooser

sparkling

un whisky (double)
uη weeskee (doobl)

a (double) whisky

un gin (-tonic)
uη djeen (-toneek)

a gin (and tonic)

sec
sehk

neat

avec des glaçons
avehk day glasoη

on the rocks

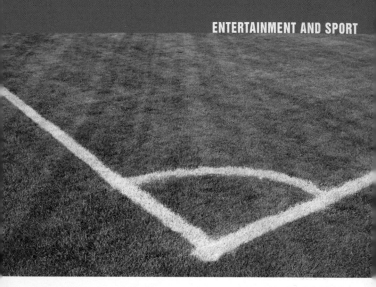

ENTERTAINMENT AND SPORT

There are many varieties of sport and entertainment to be found throughout the whole of France.

On the first page of *The Traveller in France Reference Guide*, obtainable from Maison de la France (UK tel. 09068 244123 or e-mail info@mdlf.co.uk), there is a list of 'Dates to Note' in France. Most of these are sporting or musical events. For further details, ask at your local travel agency, or contact Maison de la France (see page 22). There is an *Office de Tourisme* at 127 Champs Elysées, Paris (Metro George V), and other *Offices de Tourisme* at the main-line railway stations in Paris and all French cities. In the smaller towns, the *Syndicat d'Initiative* (SI) and the local *auberge de jeunesse* (youth hostel) will have information. Elsewhere, look for the **i** sign.

Cycling: ask at any French railway station for a list of stations from which cycles may be hired. The rates are not dear, and there are reductions for longer hire.

Cycling is not pleasant on the major roads, but the minor roads can be delightful. Some pleasant areas in which to cycle in Paris are the Bois de Boulogne and the Bois de Vincennes. Cycles may be hired from Roue Libre at 95 bis rue Rambuteau (Metro Les Halles). A useful address is The Touring Dept., Cyclists Touring Club, Cottering House, 69 Meadrow, Godalming, Surrey GU7 311S, tel. 0870 8730060.

Horse riding: travel by trekking *(randonnée à cheval)*, caravan *(roulotte)* or carriage *(calèche)* are all possible.

Canal holidays: there is a vast number of canals, providing beautiful and leisurely holidays. The *Canal du Midi* and the *Canal de Bourgogne* have many locks to negotiate, but the scenery is your reward. For the most part, no charge is made for the locks, but you are expected to help.

Running: two Parisian events are the *marathon de Paris* in spring, and the Figaro cross-country race in November.

Walking holidays *(randonnées)* are very popular in the mountainous regions of France, such as the Auvergne and the Massif Central. Details of routes can be obtained from the local *Syndicat d'Initiative*.

Son et lumière: these spectacles take place at night in places of historical interest such as the Château of Versailles. Coloured lights play upon the building to give atmosphere, while taped voices with music give an account of past events there. Occasionally live actors are used.

There are also festivals of music (classical music, opera or jazz), dance, theatre, cinema, folklore and science-fiction, and many religious celebrations throughout the year. You can buy magazines such as *Pariscope* in Paris and *Le Bulletin* in Brussels which list the current week's entertainment as well as restaurant, trips, etc.

Discos and nightclubs (*boîtes*) are to be found in most large towns. They do not generally get going until 11 pm or midnight, but often stay open until dawn. Entrance fees can be expensive, as can drinks.

One of the most popular ways of spending an evening is simply to sit on the terrace of a bar enjoying a drink with friends and watching the world go by.

Is/are there...near here?	Est-ce qu'il y a … près d'ici? *ehskeelya...preh deesee?*
...in the town	...en ville *ahη veel*
...that you recommend	...que vous pouvez recommander *ke voo poovay rekomahηday*
...a boxing match	...un match de boxe *uη match de box*
...a circus	...un cirque *uη seerk*
...a concert	...un concert *uη koηsehr*
...a disco	...une discothèque *ewn deeskotehk*
...a football match	...un match de football *uη match de fewtbohl*
...a golf course	...un terrain de golf *uη tehraη de golf*
...horse racing	...des courses de chevaux *day koors de shvoh*
...motor racing	...des courses d'auto *day koors dohtoh*
...a (musical) festival	...un festival *uη fehsteeval*

...a fun fair
...une fête foraine
ewn feht forehn

...a son-et-lumière
...un son-et-lumière
uη soη ay lewmyehr

...a sports complex
...un centre sportif
uη sahηtr sporteef

...a swimming pool (indoor)
...une piscine couverte
ewn peeseen koovehrt

...a swimming pool (outdoor)
...une piscine en plein air
ewn peeseen ahη plehnehr

...a swimming pool (heated)
...une piscine chauffée
ewn peeseen shohfay

...a skating rink
...une patinoire
ewn pateenwar

...tennis courts
...des courts de tennis
day koor de tehnees

...any walks
...des promenades
day promnad

...des randonnées
day rahηdonay

Do you like...?
Aimez-vous...?
ehmay voo...?

I like...
J'aime...
jehm...

...boxing
...la boxe
la box

...the cinema
...le cinéma
le seenayma

...concerts
...les concerts
lay koηsehr

...cricket
...le cricket
le kreekeht

...discos	...les discos *lay deeskoh*
...fishing	...la pêche *la pehsh*
...football	...le football *le fewtbohl*
...gymnastics	...la gymnastique *la jeemnasteek*
...skiing	...le ski *le skee*
...swimming	...la natation *la natasyoη*
...tennis	...le tennis *le taynees*
...walking	...les promenades *lay promnad*
...winter sports	...les sports d'hiver *lay spor deevehr*
...playing cards	...jouer aux cartes *jooay oh kart*
...playing computer games	...jouer aux jeux d'ordinateur *jooay oh jer dordeenaterr*
What does it cost to go in?	Quel est le prix d'entrée? *kehl eh le pree dahηtray?*
What is the cost per hour/ per day?	Quel est le tarif par heure/ par jour? *kehl eh le tareef par err/par joor?*
Is there tuition available?	Peut-on prendre des cours? *pertoη prahηdr day koor?*
Can I hire...?	Est-ce que je peux louer...? *ehske je per looay...?*

...a bicycle

...un vélo
un vayloh

...a tennis racquet

...une raquette de tennis
ewn rakeht de taynees

...all the equipment

...tout l'équipement
too laykeepmahn

...skis

...des skis
day skee

...skates

...des patins
day patan

BY THE SEA

Can I hire...?

Est-ce que je peux louer...?
ehske je per looay...?

...a deck chair

...une chaise longue
ewn shehz lonhg

...a motor boat

...un canot à moteur
un kanoh a moterr

...a rowing boat

...une barque
ewn bark

...a windsurfer (sailboard)

...une planche à voile
ewn plahnsh a vwal

...a surf board

...une planche de surf
ewn plahnsh de sewrf

...a swimsuit

...un maillot de bain
un mayoh de ban

...a towel

...une serviette
ewn sehrvyeht

Is it safe to swim?

Est-ce qu'on peut nager sans
danger?
ehskon per najay sahn dahnjay?

Is there a lifeguard?

Y a-t-il un surveillant de plage?
yateel un sewrveh-yahn de plaj?

Does the beach have shingle or sand?	Est-ce que la plage est de galets ou de sable? *ehske la plaj eh de galeh oo de sabl?*
When is high/low tide?	C'est quand, la marée haute/basse? *she kahη la maray oht/bas?*
Is it safe for children?	Est-ce sans danger pour les enfants? *ehs sahη dahηjay poor layz ahηfahη?*

SKIING

ski boots	des chaussures de ski *day shohsewr de skee*
ski equipment	un équipement de ski *uη aykeepmahη de skee*
skis	des skis *day skee*
a sledge	une luge *ewn lewj*
to ski	faire du ski *fehr dew skee*
skiing lessons	des leçons de ski *day lessoη de skee*
ski lift	un téléski *uη taylayskee*
ski run	une piste *ewn peest*
bindings	des fixations *day feeksasyoη*
ski pants	un fuseau *uη fewzoh*

ski sticks	des bâtons de ski *day bahton de skee*
lift pass	un forfait *un forfeh*
ski instructor	un moniteur/une monitrice *un moneeterr/ewn moneetrees*
ski jumping	le saut à skis *le soht a skee*
ski resort	une station de ski *ewn stasyon de skee*
ski slopes	des pentes de ski *day pahnt de skee*

AT THE CINEMA OR THEATRE

What's on at the cinema?	Qu'est-ce qu'il y a au cinéma? *kehskeelya ohseenayma?*
What's on at the theatre?	Qu'est-ce qu'on joue au théâtre? *kehskon joo oh tayahtr?*
Is it...?	Est-ce que c'est...? *ehske seh...?*
...an American film	...un film américain *un feelm amayreekan*
...a cartoon	...un dessin animé *un dehsan aneemay*
...a comedy	...un film comique *un feelm komeek*
...a detective film	...un film policier *un feelm poleesyay*
...a documentary	...un documentaire *un dokewmahntehr*
...a gangster film	...un film de gangsters *un feelm de gahngstehr*

...a horror film	...un film d'épouvante *uη feelm daypoovahηt*
...a romance	...un film d'amour *uη feelm damoor*
...a tragedy	...une tragédie *ewn trajaydee*
...a western	...un western *uη wehsterhrn*
...suitable for children	...pour les enfants *poor layzahηfahη*
...a new release	...une nouveauté *ewn noovohtay*
Is it...?	Est-ce qu'il est...? *ehskeel eh...?*
...in black and white	...en noir et blanc *ahη nwar ay blahη*
...dubbed	...doublé *dooblay*
...in English	...en anglais *ahn ahηgleh*
...in colour	...en couleurs *ahη koolerr*
...with the original sound track	...en version originale *ahη vehrsyoη oreejeenal*
Are there sub-titles?	Est-ce qu'il y a des sous-titres? *ehskeelya day soo teetr?*
Who's in it?	Qui joue? *kee joo?*
How much is a seat...?	Combien coûte une place...? *koηbyaη koot ewn plas...?*
...in the balcony	...au balcon *oh balkoη*

...in the stalls	...à l'orchestre *a lorkehstr* ...au parterre *oh partehr*
...near the stage	...près de la scène *preh de la sehn*
...for an adult	...pour adulte *poor adewlt*
...for a child	...pour enfant *poor ahηfahη*
Is there a special price...?	Est-ce qu'il y a un tarif spécial...? *ehskeelya uη tareef spaysyal...?*
...for children	...pour les enfants *poor layz ahηfahη*
...for a group	...pour un groupe *poor uη groop*
...for students	...pour les étudiants *poor layz aytewdyahη*
...for the unemployed	...pour les chômeurs *poor lay shohmerr*

BOOKING

I'd like...	Je voudrais... *je voodreh*
...two seats in the stalls	...deux orchestres *derz orkehstr*
...four seats together in the stalls	...quatre places ensemble au parterre *katr plas ahηsahηble oh partehr*
...a seat near the screen	...une place près de l'écran *ewn plas preh de laykrahη*
...a seat not too far back	...une place pas trop loin *ewn plas pah troh lwaη*

...a seat in the middle	...une place vers le milieu *ewn plas vehr le meelyer*
...a ticket for the afternoon performance	...un billet pour la matinée *uη beeyay poor la mateenay*
At what time does...begin/end?	A quelle heure commence/finit...? *a kehl err komahηs/feenee...?*
...the afternoon performance	...la matinée *la mateenay*
...the first performance	...la première séance *la premyehr sayahηs*
...the last performance	...la dernière séance *la dehrnyehr sayahηs*
...the interval	...l'entracte *lahηtrakt*
...half-time	...la mi-temps *la mee tahη*
Has the performance begun?	Est-ce que la séance a commencé? *ehske la sayahηs a komahηsay?*
Can we order drinks for the interval?	Est-ce qu'on peut commander des boissons pour l'entracte? *ehskoη per komahηday day bwassoη poor lahηtrakt?*
Is there a matinée performance?	Est-ce qu'il y a une matinée? *ehskeelya ewn mateenay?*
Is there a cloakroom?	Est-ce qu'il y a un vestiaire? *ehskeelya uη vestyehr?*
Where can I buy a programme?	Où est-ce que je peux acheter un programme? *oo ehske je per ashtay uη program?*

Is there access for wheelchairs?	Est-ce que les fauteuils roulants peuvent entrer? *ehske lay fohte-y roolahŋ perv ahŋtray?*

OPINIONS

What did you think of it?	Qu'est-ce que tu en as pensé? *kehske tew ahn a pahŋsay?*
It was...	Il était... *eel ayteh...*
...awful	...affreux *afrer*
...boring	...ennuyeux *ahn ŋweeyer*
...fantastic	...chouette *shooeht*
...frightening	...effrayant *ehfrayahŋ*
...funny	...amusant *amewzahŋ*
...quite interesting	...assez intéressant *assay aŋtayrehsahŋ*
...very interesting	...très intéressant *trehz aztayrehsahŋ*

YOU MAY HEAR:

il est défendu de fumer *eel eh dayfahŋdew de fewmay*	smoking not allowed
ce n'est pas permis *se neh pah pehrmee*	it is not allowed
votre billet, s'il vous plaît *votr beeay seel voo pleh*	your ticket please
programmes! *program!*	programmes!

MEETING PEOPLE

What's your name?	Comment vous appelez-vous? *komahŋ vooz aplay voo?*
My name is...	Je m'appelle... *je mapehl...*
Pleased to meet you	enchanté(e) *ahŋshahŋtay*
Is this seat free?	Est-ce que cette place est libre? *ehske seht plas eh leebr?*
Do you mind if I smoke?	Est-ce que cela vous dérange si je fume? *ehske sla voo dayrahŋj see je fewm?*
Do you have a light?	Vous avez du feu? *vooz avay dew fer?*
Would you like to...?	Voulez-vous...? *voolay voo...?*
...dance	...danser *dahŋsay*
...have something to eat/drink	...manger/boire quelque chose *maŋjay/bwar kehlk shohz*
I'm with my...	Je suis avec... *je swee avehk*
...family	...ma famille *ma famee-y*
...friends	...mes ami(e)s *mayz amee*
...boyfriend	...mon copain *moŋ kopaŋ*
...girlfriend	...ma copine *ma kopeen*

...husband	...mon mari *moη maree*
...wife	...ma femme *ma fam*
Where are you from?	D'où venez-vous? *doo venay voo?*
I'm from...	Je suis de... *je swee de...*
I'm on holiday	Je suis en vacances *je swee ahη vakahηs*
I'm studying here	Je fais des études ici *je feh dayz aytewd essee*
I'm here on business	Je suis en voyage d'affaires *je sweez ahη vwayaj daffehr*
What do you do?	Quelle est votre profession? *kehl eh votr profehsyoη?*
What are you studying?	Qu'étudiez-vous? *kaytewdyay voo?*

INTRODUCING PEOPLE

In formal society, the person who performs the introduction
between two people should speak first to the one who
commands more respect by virtue of age or sex, saying
'Madame/monsieur X, je vous présente Madame/monsieur Y.'
X says *'Enchanté(e), madame/monsieur.'* The reply from Y is
'Enchanté(e), monsieur/madam.' In informal surroundings, the
introduction goes *'Christine, voici Paul.'* Christine says *'Bonjour'*
and something like *'Ça va?'* Paul might say *'Oui,
ça va.'*

It is better not to address people over 21 as *tu* until it is clear that this is how they would like to be addressed.

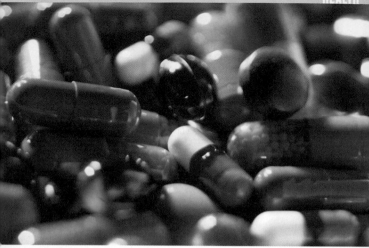

HEALTH

Before leaving for France, it is a good idea to ask at the Post Office for the form E111 to fill in and take on holiday with you. A single form will cover the whole family. If you have to pay for medical or dental attention in France, ask for a receipt *(une quittance)* for your payment. Post it with the E111 form to the regional French Health Insurance Office (ask the doctor's secretary for the address). You will eventually be sent by post up to 80% of the charges.

In order to claim money back on prescriptions, stick the price labels from the medicines on the prescription sheet.
You can top up your free health insurance with temporary health insurance from a broker's or travel agent. This usually costs very little for a short holiday.

AT THE DOCTOR'S

My...hurts	J'ai mal...
	jay mal...
...arm	...au bras
	oh bra
...back	...au dos
	oh doh
...chest	...à la poitrine
	a la pwatreen
...eyes	...aux yeux
	oh zyer
...head	...à la tête
	a la teht
...leg	...à la jambe
	a la jahηb
...stomach	...à l'estomac
	a lehstoma
...tooth	...aux dents
	oh dahη
I have asthma	J'ai de l'asthme
	jay de lasme
I am airsick	J'ai le mal de l'air
	jay le mal de lehr
I am carsick	J'ai le mal de la route
	jay le mul de la root
I am seasick	J'ai le mal de mer
	jay le mal de mehr
I have a cold	J'ai un rhume
	jay uη rewm
I am constipated	Je suis constipé
	je swee koηsteepay
I am diabetic	Je suis diabétique
	je swee deeabayteek

I have diarrhoea	J'ai la diarrhée *jay la deearay*
I have colic	J'ai la colique *jay la koleek*
I have flu	J'ai la grippe *jay la greep*
I am allergic to antibiotics/ penicillin	J'ai une allergie aux antibiotiques/à la pénicilline *jay ewn alehrjee ohz* *ahηteebeeoteek/a la* *payneeseeleen*
I have twisted my ankle	Je me suis tordu la cheville *je me swee tordew la sheveeye*
I have dizzy spells	J'ai des vertiges *jay day vehrteej*
I have a heart problem	J'ai des troubles cardiaques *jay day trooble kardeeak*
I have high blood pressure	Ma tension est trop élevée *ma tahηsyoη eh trohp aylevay*
I feel shivery	J'ai des frissons *jay day freesoη*
I have been stung by a bee/wasp	J'ai été piqué(e) par une abeille/une guêpe *jay aytay peekay par ewn* *abeh-y/ewn gehp*
I have period pains	J'ai les règles douloureuses *jay lay rehgl dooloorerz*
I feel sick	J'ai mal au coeur *jay mal oh kerr*
I have a sore throat	J'ai mal à la gorge *jay mal a la gorj*
I have a temperature	J'ai de la température/de la fièvre *jay de la tahηpayratewr/de la fyehvr*

I have sunstroke	J'ai un coup de soleil/une insolation *jay uη koo de soleh-y/ewn aηsolasyoη*
May I have a receipt?	Voulez-vous me donner un reçu *voolay voo me donay uη resew*

YOU MAY HEAR:

Je vais vous donner... *je veh voo donay...*	I'm going to give you...
...une piqûre *ewn peekewr*	...an injection
...cette crème *seht krehm*	...this cream
...ce médicament *se maydeekamahη*	...this medicine
...ce sirop *se seeroh*	...this mixture
...une ordonnance *ewn ordonahηs*	...a prescription
...ces pilules/ces cachets *say peelewl/say kashay*	...these pills
Allez au lit tout de suite *alay oh lee tout sweet*	Go to bed straight away
Gardez le lit pendant...jours *garday le lee pahηdahη... joor*	Stay in bed for...days
Allez chez le dentiste *alay shay le dahηteest*	Go to the dentist
Allez chez l'opticien *alay shay lopteesyaη*	Go to the optician
Qu'est-ce qu'il y a? *kehskeelya?*	What's the matter?

Où est-ce que vous avez mal? *oo ehske vooz avay mal?*	Where does it hurt?
Il faut prendre un médicament *eel foh prahηdr uη maydeekamahη*	You must take some medicine

I've been in pain,...	J'ai mal depuis... *jay mal depwee...*
...for a week	...une semaine *ewn smehn*
...for several days	...plusieurs jours *plewzyerr joor*
...since yesterday	...hier *yehr*
...since this morning	...ce matin *se mataη*
...for a few hours	...quelques heures *kehlkez err*
I had the same problem	J'ai eu le même problème... *jay ew le mehm problehm...*
...last year	...l'année dernière *lanay dernyehr*
...a few years ago	...il y a quelques années *eelya kehlkezanay*
...two months ago	...il y a deux mois *eelya der mwa*

AT THE DENTIST'S

Is that the dentist's waiting room?	C'est bien la salle d'attente du dentiste? *seh byan la sal datahηt dew dahηteest?*
Can I have an appointment with ...	Est-ce que je peux prendre rendez-vous avec...s'il vous plaît? *ehske je per prahndr rahηday voo avehk...seel voo pleh?*

When is his surgery?

A quelle heure consulte-t-il?
a kehl err koŋsewlt teel?

I have toothache

J'ai un mal de dents
jay uŋ mal de dahŋ

I'm insured

Je suis assuré(e)
je swee asewray

My filling's come out

Mon plombage a sauté
moŋ plombaj a sohtay

YOU MAY HEAR:

Qu'est-ce qu'il y a?
kehskeelya?

What's the matter?

Il consulte cet après-midi
eel koŋsewlt seht apreh meedee

There is a surgery this afternoon

Est-ce que vous avez mal?
ehske vooz avay mal?

Are you in pain?

Est-ce que vous pouvez venir dans une heure?
ehske voo poovay veneer dahŋz ewn err?

Can you come in an hour?

Quel est votre nom?
kehl eh votr noŋ?

What's your name?

Vous êtes assuré(e)?
vooz eht asewray?

Are you insured?

Quelle dent vous fait mal?
kehl dahŋ voo feh mal?

Which tooth hurts?

AT THE CHEMIST'S

May I have...

Est-ce que je peux avoir...
ehske je per avwar...

...an (antiseptic) cream

...une crème (antiseptique)
ewn krehm ahŋteesehpteek

...some aspirin

...a bandage

...some cream

...a lotion

...some medicine

...a mixture

...a prescription

...these pills

...some sticking-plaster

Could you make up this prescription?

Do you have anything for...?

...de l'aspirine
de laspeereen

...un pansement
uη pahηsmahη

...de la crème
de la krehm

...une lotion
ewn lohsyoη

...un médicament
uη maydeekamahη

...un sirop
uη seeroh

...une ordonnance
ewn ordonahηs

...ces pilules
say peelewl

...ces cachets
say kashay

...du sparadrap
dew sparadra

Voulez-vous préparer cette ordonnance?
voolay voo prayparay seht ordonahηs?

Avez-vous quelque chose contre...?
avay voo kehlke shohz koηtr...?

AT THE OPTICIAN'S

I've broken my glasses

Can you repair them?

J'ai cassé mes lunettes
jay kassay may lewneht

Pouvez-vous les réparer?
poovay voo lay rayparay?

When will they be ready?	Quand seront-elles prêtes? *kahη seroηtehl preht?*
Can you change the lenses?	Pouvez-vous changer les verres? *poovay voo shahηjay lay vehr?*
I'd like a case for my glasses	Je voudrais un étui à lunettes *je voodreh uη aytwee a lewneht*
I've lost one of my contact lenses	J'ai perdu un verre de contact *jay pehrdew uη vehr de koηtakt*
Have you any contact lens cleaning liquid?	Avez-vous un produit pour nettoyer les verres de contact? *avay voo un prodwee poor nehtwayay lay vehr de koηtakt?*
I have hard/soft lenses	J'ai des verres de contact durs/souples *jay day vehr de koηtakt dewr/soopl*
I'm short-sighted/long-sighted	Je suis myope/presbyte *jswee myop/prehsbeet*
I need some sunglasses	Il me faut des lunettes de soleil *eel me foh day lewneht de soleh-y*

YOU MAY HEAR:

Portez-vous des verres de contact durs ou souples? *portay voo day vehr de koηtakt dewr oo soopl?*	Do you wear hard or soft contact lenses?

DRIVING

There are rules differing from British regulations regarding
car insurance, driving in winter, motorcycles, motorways,
parking, fines, speed limits, road signs, etc.
Motorists who purchase European Motoring Assistance from
the RAC (tel. 0800 550 055) or 'Five Star Europe'
insurance from the AA (tel. 0800 085 7261) will receive also
some general European motoring information.
If you wish to know about less crowded routes through
France, ask for the English language version of the *Bison-Futé*

There are some surprising differences between French
and English requirements and habits. For example, if a
driver flashes you he expects you to pull aside and let
him pass.

brochure, available from toll booths and motorway service stations in France, or from the French Tourist Office (Maison de La France), 178 Piccadilly, London W1J 9AL, tel. 0906 824 4123.

ROAD INFORMATION

Your travel agent will be able to give you information about vehicle insurance (including Green Cards), lights, mirrors, nationality plates, age limits, police fines (which can be immediate and extremely high), seat belts, snow chains, warning triangles, hazard warning lights, etc. If you purchase insurance you receive more detailed information which includes a selection of continental road signs, a table covering the speed limits in various countries, and detailed advice on emergency services.

USEFUL ROAD SIGNS

priority road
(even if there are no other signs)

end of priority road
(usually on entering
urban zone)

All drivers must carry:
* passport or identity card
* driver's licence *(permis de conduire)*
* car ownership papers *(carte grise* - grey card)
* proof of third-party insurance *(carte verte* - green card).

There are various types of road:

- *Autoroutes* (motorways) are shown by the letter A on blue and white road signs. Tolls are usually exacted.
- *Routes Nationales* (main highways) have the prefix N or RN.
- *Routes Départementales* (local roads) have the prefix D.
- *Routes Communales* (minor roads) sometimes have the prefix C or V.

The less crowded routes have green and white road signs.

You may see the following phrases on the road signs:

The side of the street on which you may park varies, so it is best to imitate the local drivers.

allumez vos phares	**switch on your lights**
attention au feu	**fire hazard**
attention travaux	**beware road works**
barrière de dégel	**road closed to lorries when ice is thawing**
chaussée déformée	**uneven road surface**
fin d'interdiction de parking	**end of prohibited parking**
gravillons	**loose chippings**
haute tension	**electrified line**
interdit aux piétons	**forbidden to pedestrians**
nids de poules	**potholes**
rappel	**remember! (displayed on speed limit signs)**
route barrée	**road closed**

USEFUL ROAD SIGNS

Parking: large towns have the usual car parks and parking meters. However, smaller towns may have a system whereby you display a blue disc *(un disque de contrôle)* in the Blue Zones (*Zones Bleues*). This is obtainable free from Tourist Offices, garages or tobacconists. On it you indicate the time you parked. You are allowed one hour between 9–12.30 and 14.30–19.00.

Driving licence, registration and insurance papers: up-to-date documents for these must be taken with you on holiday, and be readily available for the police. A valid British driving licence will suffice in France, but if you intend to travel in other countries, it may be advisable to obtain an International Driving Permit, details of which are available from British motoring organisations such as the AA and RAC (see page 74).

Insurance: although insurance policies issued in the UK and the Republic of Ireland automatically provide minimum cover in EU countries, the overseas cover will satisfy only the minimum legal requirement, and it is quite possible that your cover will be less than in the UK. It is therefore advisable to consult your insurer, who will issue an International Green Card to extend your UK cover.

If you are travelling through France to Spain, it is worth asking your insurer about a Bail Bond.

Basic 3rd party insurance cover is available at the main frontier posts.

MAXIMUM SPEED LIMITS

	normal weather	rain or poor visibility
built-up areas	50 km/h (31 mph)	50 km/h (31 mph)

*Some important through roads allow 70 km/h (43mph) through
towns.*

outside built-up areas (includes dual carriageways)	90 km/h (56 mph)	80 km/h (50 mph)

*If separated by a central reservation,
the upper limit on dual carriageways is:*

	110 km/h (68 mph)	100 km/h (62 mph)
motorways	130 km/h (81 mph)	110 km/h (68 mph)
urban sections of motorway	110 km/h (68 mph)	100 km/h (62 mph)
on the Paris ring road	80 km/h (50 mph)	

Certain credit cards including Visa are now accepted on French
autoroutes. Motorways are toll-free in Belgium. In Switzerland
you have to display a special motorway tax sticker. This is
available in Britain through the motoring organisations, or you
can buy it at the Swiss frontier.

Note: The above should be taken as no more than a general guide. There are further restrictions on motorcyclists, on motorists who have held a driving licence for less than two years and on cars towing a caravan or trailer. Detailed advice should be sought.

Tolls *(péage)*: the autoroutes (prefixed A on the road signs) are toll-operated except for their urban sections. This means you must be ready to halt and pay the appropriate charge (in euros) shortly after you see a sign such as

either by paying the attendant or by throwing the correct money into a special collection net.
The toll-booths can supply free maps of less crowded roads, which do not require tolls. Some British motoring organisations offer similar maps, or recommended routes specially prepared to your own requirements.

 You may find country garages shut between 12 and 2 pm. Credit cards are not always accepted in payment for petrol, so make sure you have sufficient euros with you.

CONVERSION TABLES

Distance e.g. 10 km = 6 miles, 10 miles = 16 km

miles	6	12	19	25	31	37	44
km/mile	10	20	30	40	50	60	70
km	16	32	48	64	80	97	113

miles	50	56	62	68	75	81
km/mile	80	90	100	110	120	130
km	129	145	161	177	194	210

AT A GARAGE OR PETROL STATION

Buying petrol

Essence, *essence normale* or *essence ordinaire* all refer to regular petrol.

- *Essence super* is premium petrol.
- Unleaded petrol is *sans plomb*.
- Leaded petrol has been withdrawn.
- Lead Replacement Petrol (LRP) is *supercarburant*.
- Liquid Petroleum Gas (LPG) is available from certain petrol stations. For a map call 0033 1 41 97 02 80.

Where's the nearest petrol station?	Où se trouve la station-service la plus proche? *oo se troov la stasyon sehrvees la plew prosh?*
Do you accept credit cards?	Est-ce que vous acceptez les cartes de crédit? *ehske vooz aksehptay lay kart de kraydee?*
Fill the tank, please	Faites le plein, s'il vous plaît *feht le plan, seel voo pleh*
Give me…litres of regular/ premium	Donnez-moi…litres d'ordinaire/de super *donay mwa…leetr dordeenehr/desewpehr*

Give me...euros worth of 2 star/4 star, please	Donnez-moi de l'ordinaire/du super pour...euros, s'il vous plaît *donay mwa de lordeenehr/ dew sewpehr poor...erroh seel voo pleh*
How much is it a litre?	C'est combien le litre? *seh koηbyaη le leetr?*
I'll have the 4 star/unleaded, please	Je prends le super/sans plomb s'il vous plaît *je prahη le sewpehr/sahη ploη seel voo pleh*
Will you check the oil too?	Voulez-vous aussi vérifier l'huile? *voolay voo ohsee vayreefyay lweel?*
Have you a road map?	Avez-vous une carte routière? *avay voo ewn kart rootyehr?*
How much do I owe you?	Je vous dois combien? *je voo dwa koηbyaη?*
How far is it to the motorway?	L'autoroute est à quelle distance? *lohtohroot eht a kehl deestahηs?*
May we use the toilets?	Est-ce qu'on peut se servir des toilettes? *ehskoη per se sehrveer day twaleht?*
Do you have air for the tyres?	Avez-vous de l'air pour les pneus? *avay voo de lehr poor lay pner?*
Is there any water?	Y a-t-il de l'eau? *yateel de loh?*
I'd like a litre of oil	Je voudrais un litre d'huile *je voodreh uη leetr dweel*
Will you check...	Voulez-vous vérifier... *voolay voo vayreefyay...*

...the brakes	...les freins *lay fraη*
...the oil	...l'huile *lweel*
...the tyres	...les pneus *lay pner*
...the spare wheel	...la roue de secours *la roo de skoor*
...the water	...l'eau *loh*
...the tyre pressure	...la pression des pneus *la prehsyoη day pner*
attendant	le/la pompiste *le/la poηpeest*
cash desk	la caisse *la kehs*
to check	vérifier *vayreefyay*
to clean	nettoyer *nehtwayay*
to inflate	gonfler *goηflay*
petrol	l'essence *lehsahηs*
regular	ordinaire *ordeenehr*
premium	super *sewpehr*
road map	la carte routière *la kart rootyehr*

YOU MAY HEAR:

Allez tout droit *alay too drwa*	Go straight on
C'est à cent mètres *sehta sahη mehtr*	It's 100 metres away
C'est loin *seh lwaη*	It's a long way
C'est là-bas *seh la bah*	It's over there
Super ou ordinaire? *sewpehr oo ordeenehr?*	Do you want premium or regular?
Le super est à...le litre *le sewpehr ehta...le leetr*	The premium is...a litre
C'est tout? *seh too?*	Is that all?
Il faut aller à la caisse *eel foh alay a la kehs*	You'll have to go to the cash desk
Nous n'en avons pas pour cette marque *noo nahηavoη pah poor seht mark*	We haven't got any for that make
Vous avez la clef, s'il vous plaît? *vooz avay la klay seel voo pleh?*	Do you have the key, please?

A CAR BREAKDOWN

What's the matter?	Qu'est-ce qu'il y a? *kehskeelya?*

In case of need, if your car is one of the following makes you can phone to ask where the nearest service station is: Peugeot 00800 83 89 13 19; Renault 01 41 04 54 05 or 08 10 40 50 60; Citroën 0 800 05 24 24 (free) or 0810 63 90 00 *numéro Azur* 3615 CITROËN.

My car is a Citroën/Renault/Peugeot	Ma voiture est une Citroën/Renault/Peugeot *ma vwatewr ehtewn seetrerη/renoh/perjoh*
My car's broken down	Je suis tombé(e) en panne *je swee toηbay ahη pan*
Where is the nearest service station for Citroëns/Renaults/Peugeots?	Où est la station-service la plus proche pour les Citroëns/Renaults/Peugeots? *oo eh la stasyoη sehrvees la plew prosh poor lay seetrerη/renoh/perjoh?*
The car is near Nancy/Nice/Nantes	La voiture est près de Nancy/Nice/Nantes *La vwatewr eh preh de nahηsee/nees/nahηt*
I've run out of petrol	Je suis en panne d'essence *je swee ahη pan dehsahηs*
I've got a puncture	J'ai un pneu crevé *jay ew uη pner krevay*
Can you come?	Pouvez-vous venir? *poovay voo vneer?*
I was rammed by...	J'ai été embouti(e) par... *jay aytay ahηbootee par...*
I bumped into...	J'ai embouti... *jay ahηbootee...*
...the car	...la voiture *la vwatewr*
...the lorry	...le camion *le kamyoη*
...the motor-bike	...la moto *la motoh*
...the pedestrian	...le piéton *le pyaytoη*

I am insured	Je suis assuré(e)
	je swee asewray
Can you repair the...?	Pouvez-vous réparer...?
	poovay voo rayparay...?
The...isn't working	...ne marche pas
	ne marsh pah
...battery	...la batterie
	la batree
...brakes	...les freins
	lay fran
...door	...la portière
	la portyehr
...exhaust	...l'échappement
	layshapmahn
...fan belt	...la courroie de ventilateur
	la koorwa de vahnteelaterr
...headlights	...les phares
	lay far
...indicator	...le clignotant
	le kleenyotahn
...radiator	...le radiateur
	le radyaterr
...seat belt	...la ceinture de sécurité
	la santewr de saykewreetay
...spare wheel	...la roue de secours
	la roo de skoor
...steering wheel	...le volant
	le volahn
...window	...la glace
	la glas
...windscreen	...le pare-brise
	le par breez

TRAVELLING AROUND

All enquiries about travel to France may be addressed to Maison de la France, 178 Piccadilly, London W1J 9AL. Their brochure, *The Traveller in France Reference Guide*, is a mine of information about all aspects of holidaying in France, including travel (please enclose minimum of £1 in postage stamps).

Alternatively, phone their France Information Line (09068 244123), or ask either by e-mail from info@mdlf.co.uk or via the Web (www.franceguide.com). The travel section of *The Traveller in France Reference Guide* describes all aspects of travel from the UK to France and within France, with many addresses and phone, fax and e-mail numbers given.

Another useful website is www.france.tourism.com, supplied by the French Government Tourist office.

HITCH-HIKING

Hitch-hiking (*l'autostop*) has more official recognition in France than in Britain. However, with all hitch-hiking, caution is advised, especially for women. A safer form of hitch-hiking is perhaps 'ride-share'.

RIDE-SHARE

AllostopProvoya (website www.ecritel.fr/allostop, e-mail allostop@ecritel.fr) matches would-be travellers and drivers. There is an administrative fee.

CAR RENTAL

It is usually cheaper to rent a car from an English agency or to use a purchase-repurchase plan (see below). Some car hire agencies in England are as follows:

www.avis.co.uk (tel. 08700 100287)

www.europcar.com (tel. 0870 607 5000 for reservations, e-mail reservationsuk@mail.europcar.com for both enquiries and reservations)

www.executive-car.com (tel. 0033 1 42 65 54 29)
www.hertz.co.uk (tel. 0208 679 0181)
www.nationalcar.com (tel. 08705 365 365)
Budget Leisure car (tel. 08701 56 56 56)
Thrifty (tel. 08705 168 238)

You can enquire about fly-drive arrangements either through your airline or your tour operator.

In France, a list of local car hire agencies may be obtained at local tourist offices (called *Syndicat d'Initiative* or SI). Or you can ask at the local French railway station for *un pliant sur la location des voitures*.

If you need a car for a month or more, you could enquire into the purchase-repurchase *(achat-rachat)* plans offered by such makes as Peugeot and Renault. These offer considerable savings on renting.

Where is the car rental agency?	Où se trouve l'agence de location de voitures? *oo se troov lajahηs de lokasyoη de vwatewr?*
I'd like to hire a car...	Je voudrais louer une voiture... *je voodreh looay ewn vwatewr...*
...for one/two/three people	...pour une/deux/trois personne(s) *poor ewn/der/trwa pehrson*
...for a day/a week	...pour un jour/une semaine *poor uη joor/ewn smehn*

It may be possible to hire a car in advance to await your arrival at your train destination.

What are your charges per day/per kilometre?	Quels sont vos tarifs par jour/par kilomètre? *kel soη voh tareef par joor/par keelomehtr?*
How much is the insurance/deposit?	Combien coûte l'assurance/la caution? *koηbyaη koot lasewrahηs/la kohsyoη?*
Will you write it down, please?	Voulez-vous l'écrire, s'il vous plaît? *voolay voo laykreer, seel voo pleh?*
What is the total cost?	Quel est le montant? *kehl eh le moηtaη?*
Is it air-conditioned?	Est-ce qu'elle est climatisée? *ehskehl eh kleemateezay?*
Is there a radio?	Est-ce qu'il y a une radio? *ehskeelya ewn radyoh?*

TAKING A TAXI

Where can I find a taxi?	Où est-ce que je peux trouver un taxi? *oo ehske je per troovay uη taxee?*
I want to go to...	Je veux aller à... *je ver alay a...*
...the airport	...l'aéroport *la-ayropor*
...the hotel	...l'hôtel *lohtehl*
...the station	...la gare *la gar*
How much is it?	C'est combien? *seh koηbyaη?*
It's near here	C'est près d'ici *seh preh deesee*

Will you...?	Voulez-vous...?
	voolay voo... ?
...carry my bags	...porter mes bagages
	portay may bagaj
...slow down	...ralentir
	ralahηteer
...stop here	...vous arrêter ici
	vooz arehtay eesee
...wait for me	...m'attendre
	matahηdr

TRAVEL BY AIR

For information about flights to all areas and by different airlines, the following websites and telephone numbers are useful:
www.airfrance.com or www.airfrance.co.uk (tel. Paris 01 41 56 78 00 or London 0845 0845 111)
www.aurigny.com (tel. 01481 822886)
AOM French Airlines (tel. 01293 596663)
www.britishairways.com (tel. 0845 77 333 77)
www.britishmidland.com (tel. 0870 6070 555)
www.govoyages.com (tel. 01 53 40 44 29)
www.look-voyages.fr (tel. 01 55 49 49 60)
Low cost airlines are as follows:
www.easyjet.com (tel. 0870 6000 000)
www.ryanair.com (tel. 08701 569 569)

Within France

Air France has an extensive domestic air network. For reservations in the UK, call Air France Reservations (tel. 0845 0845 111).

In Paris

The two main airports are as follows:
Orly airport (tel. 01 49 75 15 15). From here there are planes to 34 destinations in France. In addition, there are the *Navettes*. These planes operate from Orly West airport to Nice, Marseilles and

Toulouse every 30 minutes, and to Bordeaux every hour. From Orly
there are buses to the Invalides and Montparnasse.
Trains run to the Gare d'Austerlitz and Saint-Michel.
Roissy Charles de Gaulle airport (tel. 01 48 62 22 80) sends planes
to 18 destinations in France. The name is often abbreviated to **Paris
CDG** (pronounced *say day jay*). There are buses to a point fairly near
the Champs-Elysées, and trains to the Gare du Nord and Châtelet-
Les Halles.

What flight must I get to go to Brussels?	Pour aller à Bruxelles je dois prendre quel vol? *poor alay a brewsehl je dwa prahŋdr kehl vol?*
What time is the next flight to London?	A quelle heure est le prochain vol pour Londres? *a kehl err eh le proshaŋ vol poor loŋdr?*
Do I have to change planes?	Est-ce qu'il faut changer d'avion? *ehskeel foh shahŋjay davyoŋ?*
Where (do I have to do that)?	Où ça? *oo sa?*
From which airport?	De quel aéroport? *de kehl a-ayropor?*
From which air terminal?	De quelle aérogare? *de kehl a-ayrogar?*
Where is the departure lounge?	Où se trouve la salle de départ? *oo se troov la sal de daypar?*
What is the departure time?	Quelle est l'heure de départ? *kehl eh lerr de daypar?*

Where is the duty-free shop?	Où se trouve le magasin hors-taxe? *oo se troov le magazan or tax?*
Is the flight delayed?	Est-ce que le vol est en retard? *ehske le vol ehtahn retar?*
When do I have to check in?	Quand est-ce qu'il faut s'enregistrer? *kahntehskeel foh sahnrejeestray?*
Is there a bus to the airport/ town centre?	Y a-t-il un bus à l'aéroport/au centre-ville? *yateel un bews a la-ayropor/oh sahntr-veel?*
I'd like a seat...	J'aimerais un siège/une place... *jehmereh un syehj/ewn plas*
...by the window	...à côté de la fenêtre *a kohtay de la fnehtr*
...near the aisle	...près du couloir *preh dew koolwar*
...at the back	...à l'arrière *a laryehr*

TRAVEL BY TRAIN

The French train network is known as the SNCF *(Société Nationale des Chemins de fer Français)*. French trains are modern, speedy and comfortable, with connecting bus and coach services to all parts of France.

As well as the savings offered by French Railpass and InterRail, there are reductions available for children, young people and senior citizens, also for off-peak travel (marked in blue on the SNCF timetables). Most main-line trains add a supplement to their fares

 With the exception of Eurostar, before you board the train you must date-stamp your ticket and reservation in one of the orange machines on the platform. Otherwise you will have to pay a fee.

for peak-time travel (marked in red on the SNCF timetables).

For information about these reductions and other details about train travel to and within France, the following websites and telephone numbers are useful:

For Eurostar (with additional services to Disneyland, Paris), TGV, French Railpass, Inter-Rail or French Motorail:

www.raileurope.co.uk (tel. 08705 848 848), The Rail Europe Travel Centre, 178 Piccadilly, London W1J 9BA. Rail Europe is the UK subsidiary of the SNCF.

For Motorail bookings: www.frenchmotorail.com (tel. 08702 415 415).

It is inadvisable to buy your ticket on the train from the ticket collector (*contrôleur*), as you will be charged at the full rate plus rather a hefty fee. When asking the way to the correct platform, it is better to ask *C'est quelle voie, s'il vous plaît?* (Which track?) than *C'est quel quai, s'il vous plaît?* (Which platform?) because there are two *voies* (tracks) to each *quai* (platform).

Is there a special price...?	Est-ce qu'il y a un tarif spécial...? *ehskeelya uη tareef spaysyal...?*
...today	...aujourd'hui *ohjoordwee*
...for children	...pour les enfants *poor layz ahηfahη*
...for senior citizens	...pour les personnes âgées *poor lay pehrsonzahjay*
A ticket for...please	Un billet pour...s'il vous plaît *uη beeyay poor...seel voo pleh*
A single	Un aller *ern alay*
A return	Un aller-retour *ern alay retoor*
first class	première classe *premyehr klas*

second class	seconde classe *zegoηd klas*
How much is that?	C'est combien? *seh koηbyaη?*
What time does the train leave?	Le train part à quelle heure? *le traη par a kehl err?*
Do I have to change?	Est-ce qu'il faut changer? *ehskeel foh shahηjay?*
How long does it take?	Il faut mettre combien de temps pour arriver? *eel foh mehtr koηbyaη de tahη poor areevay?*
Is this the right train for...?	C'est bien le train pour...? *seh byaη le traη poor...?*
Is this seat free?	Est-ce que cette place est libre? *ehske seht plas eh leebr?*
I'm sorry/excuse me	Pardon *pardoη*
Which...is it to go to Calais?	Pour aller à Calais c'est quel(le)... *poor allay a kaleh seh kehl...?*
...counter	...guichet *geeshay*
...train	...train *traη*
...exit	...sortie *sortee*
...entrance	...entrée *ahηtray*
...seat	...place *plas*

Note: there are two *voies* on each *quai*. It is better to ask for the *voie* than the *quai*.

...station	...gare *gar*
...platform	...quai *keh*
...track/platfrom	...voie *vwa*
Which platform does the train leave from?	Le train part de quelle voie? *le traη par de kehl vwa?*
At what time does the train for ...leave?	A quelle heure part le train pour...? *a kehl err par le traη poor...?*

YOU MAY HEAR:

Un aller simple ou un aller-retour? *ern alay sahηpl oo ern alayretoor?*	Single or return?
Première classe ou seconde classe? *premyehr klas oo zegoηd klas?*	1st or 2nd class?
Non, c'est un train direct *noη seht uη traη deerehkt*	No, it's a through train
De la voie numéro dix *de la vwa newmayroh dees*	From platform 10
Toutes les vingt minutes *toot lay vahη meenewt*	Every 20 minutes
occupé *okewpay*	taken
Votre billet, s'il vous plaît *votr beeyay seel voo pleh*	Could I see your ticket, please?
Il faut changer à... *eel foh shahηjay a...*	You have to change at...

TRAVEL BY BUS OR COACH

To reach France

A useful website is:

www.gobycoach.com (address Eurolines Travel Shop, 52 Grosvenor Gardens, London SW1W 0AU).

National Express can provide connections to the Eurolines from all parts of the UK (tel. 08705 143 219).

Within France

In France, information about local buses may be obtained at the local tourist office (called *Syndicat d'Initiative*, abbreviated to SI). Information on coaches and buses that complement the rail network may be obtained from SNCF stations and offices.

In Paris

Bus travel in Paris is surprisingly easy, especially if you ask at any main-line Metro or bus station for a free *Plan de Paris* (or *carte du réseau*). *(Pouvez-vous me donner un Plan de Paris, s'il vous plaît?)* This shows bus routes as well as Metro and RER routes. www.ratp.fr is a useful website. Telephone 0 836 68 41 41 14 for information in English about Paris transport by bus and Metro.

Reduced fares in Paris

You can buy from a Metro station or bus terminus a booklet (*carnet*) of ten *Métro-Autobus* tickets, which you can share with your friends. There are also special offers such as *Carte Orange* (for which you need a passport-sized photograph), a *Paris Visite* ticket or a *Mobilis* card and coupon. The *Carte Orange* is the cheapest and easiest of the three. They can be bought not only at Metro and bus stations in Paris, but also from specialist travel agents or from Voyages Vacances International (address The Linen Hall, 162-168 Regent Street, W1R 5TB).

See the section in this book on the Metro (pages 97-99) for more detailed information.

It is possible to buy a ticket at an SNCF station in the outskirts of Paris to include travel on the Paris Metro and buses. If in doubt whether in-Paris travel is included, it is better to ask *('Est-ce que le Métro est compris?').*

Night buses in Paris – the Noctambus
The Noctambus costs nothing if you have a *Paris Visite* pass, a *Mobilis* card or a *Carte Orange* for the zone you are in. Even if you have not, prices are very reasonable. Buses run once an hour. The bus stops may be recognised by the sign of a black owl silhouetted against a quarter moon.

I'd like a leaflet about excursions, please	Je voudrais un dépliant sur les excursions, s'il vous plaît *je voodreh uη daypleeahη sewr layz ehkskewrzyoη, seel voo pleh*
Is there a bus or coach for Paris tomorrow?	Est-ce qu'il y a un bus ou un car pour Paris demain? *ehskeelya uη bews oo uη kar poor paree demaη?*
I'd like to book two seats	Je voudrais réserver deux places *je voodreh raysehrvay der plas*
a single	un aller *ern alay*
a return	un aller-retour *ern alay retoor*
When do we arrive in Bordeaux?	On arrive à Bordeaux à quelle heure? *oη areev a bordoh a kehl err?*
Where do we get on the bus?	Où est-ce qu'on prend le bus? *oo ehskoη prahη le bews?*

Is the bus station near here?	Est-ce que la gare routière est près d'ici? *ehske la gar rootyehr eh preh deesee?*
How often is the bus?	Il y a un bus tous les combien? *eelya uηbews too lay koηbyaη?*
Where is the bus stop?	Où est l'arrêt, s'il vous plaît? *oo eh lareh, seel voo pleh?*
Which bus stop does the bus/coach for Marseilles leave from?	L'autobus/le car pour Marseille part de quel arrêt? *lohtobews/le kar poor marseh-y par de kehl areh?*

TRAVEL ON THE METRO

Several bargains are offered to the Metro traveller. Free maps may be obtained at Metro ticket windows. Reduced fares are available. The following two offers may be used interchangeably on Metro, bus and RER within Paris:

1. a *Carte Orange*, valid for bus/Metro/RER, may be obtained at any Metro or RER ticket window, or in shops displaying the RATP or *Carte Orange* logo. To be able to travel with it, buy a coupon for the correct number of zones (usually Zones 1 and 2 will be suitable, unless you intend to travel outside the suburbs). Choose a coupon either for one week *(pour une semaine)* or for one month *(pour un mois)*. The weekly ticket is valid from Monday to Sunday, and the monthly ticket starts at the beginning of each month. You must write your name on the *Carte Orange*, and the number of your *Carte*

Paris Visite passes are particularly suitable for tourists, as they include discounts on some museum admissions, etc. They vary in price according to how many days' validity they have, and in how many zones you wish to travel.

Orange on each coupon. It is not transferable. A passport-sized photo is needed. Do not punch your coupons. Simply show the card. The stops on the RER are further apart than those on the Metro. On the RER you may travel only within Zone 1 with a *Carte Orange* coupon.

2. a booklet *(un carnet)* of ten tickets for Metro, buses and trams. Punch your own ticket as you enter the bus/tram or pass the Metro barrier, and keep it until you have finished your journey. If you arrive on Saturday, you could buy a *carnet* to share with a friend to last until Monday, when your weekly *Carte Orange* becomes valid. On the RER you may travel only within Zone 1 with one of these tickets. You cannot transfer from the Metro to a bus or vice versa with a single ticket, or between buses.

Validate your tickets by punching (*composter*). DO NOT PUNCH the *Carte Orange*, *Paris Visite* or *Mobilis* pass, or you will not be able to use them again. However, if you are travelling to the suburbs on a full-sized SNCF ticket, this should be punched, or if you use one ticket from a *carnet*. If in doubt, ask '*Est-ce qu'il faut composter?*'

FINDING YOUR WAY ON THE METRO

Each line (*ligne*) has two directions (*directions*). To find your direction, follow your line through on the map of the Metro from the station where you are, through the station you want to go to, to the end of the line. The last station on the line is the name of your direction. Imagine you are at the Gare du Nord in the following diagram:

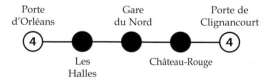

Porte d'Orléans — (4) — Les Halles — Gare du Nord — Château-Rouge — (4) — Porte de Clignancourt

For Les Halles, you need *ligne 4, direction Porte d'Orléans.*
For Château-Rouge you need *ligne 4, direction Porte de Clignancourt.*

I'd like a booklet of tickets and a plan	Je voudrais un carnet de tickets et un plan *je voodreh un karnay de teekay ay un plahn*
the automatic barrier	le portillon automatique *le porteeyon otomateek*
the (Metro) train	la rame *la ram*
the (Metro) station	la station *la stasyon*
Is it necessary to change trains to get to Versailles?	Pour aller à Versailles faut-il changer de train? *poor alay a vehrsa-y fohteel shahnjay de tran?*
Which direction must I get?	Je dois prendre quelle direction? *je dwa prahndr kehl deerehksyon?*
Where must I get a connection?	Où faut-il prendre une correspondance? *oo fohteel prahndr ewn korehspondahns?*

YOU MAY SEE:

Accès aux Quais	to the platforms
Entrée	entrance
Sortie	exit
Interdit de fumer	no smoking
Place reservée aux femmes enceintes, aux handicapés et aux mutilés de guerre	seat reserved for pregnant women, disabled people and disabled ex-servicemen

SHOPPING

Shops are generally open between 9 am and 5.30 pm or later, although post offices open at 8 am, and *boulangeries* at 7.30 or 8 am. Some hypermarkets do not close until 10 pm.

In Belgium shops tend to close at 6 pm. In Switzerland they close at 6.30 pm Monday to Friday, and at 5 pm on Saturdays.

 Smaller shops often close during the lunch hour. Two hours is not uncommon, and in some parts lunch hours have been known to stretch to four hours. Many shops are closed on Mondays as well as Sundays.

Butcher's shops: a *charcuterie* sells pork products, and a *boucherie* sells non-pork products.

Stamps can be bought not only at the post offices, but also at the supermarkets, shops that sell postcards, and the *tabacs* (easily spotted by the cigar-shaped sign outside).

You can find high-quality goods at very reasonable prices in Paris at the large department stores *(les grands magasins)* such as Le Printemps (metro Havre Caumartin), Galeries Lafayette (metro Auber), La Samaritaine (metro Pont Neuf) and Bazar de l'Hôtel de Ville (metro Hôtel de Ville).

I'm looking for...	Je cherche... *je shehrsh*
I'm just looking	Je ne fais que regarder *je ne feh ke regarday*
Can you show me...?	Pouvez-vous me montrer...? *poovay voo me moηtray...?*
Where do I pay?	Où se trouve la caisse? *oo se troov la kehs?*
Please write it down	Pouvez-vous l'écrire, s'il vous plaît? *poovay voo laykreer, seel voo pleh*
I don't want to spend more than ...euros	Je ne veux pas dépenser plus de...euros *je ne ver pah daypahηsay plew de...erroh*
Can I order it?	Est-ce que je peux le commander? *ehske je per le komahηday?*
Do you accept credit cards?	Acceptez-vous les cartes de crédit? *aksehptay voo lay kart de kraydee?*

Can I pay by traveller's cheque?	Est-ce que je peux payer avec un chèque de voyage? *ehske je per payay avehk un shehk de vwayaj?*
Do I have to pay VAT?	Dois-je payer le TVA? *dwaj payay le tay vay a?*
Where is the...	Où est... *oo eh...*
...baker's	...la boulangerie *la boolahnjree*
...bookshop	...la librairie *la leebrehree*
...butcher's	...la boucherie *la booshree*
...café & tobacconist's	...le café-tabac *le kafay taba*
...cake shop	...la pâtisserie *la pahteesree*
...chemist's/drugstore	...la pharmacie *la farmasee*
...dairy	...la crèmerie *la krehmree*
...delicatessen/pork butcher's	...la charcuterie *la sharkewtree*
...fish shop	...la poissonnerie *la pwasonree*
...fruiterer	...le marchand de fruits *le marshahn de frwee*
...grocer's	...l'alimentation/l'épicerie *laleemahntasyon/laypeesree*
...newspaper kiosk	...le kiosque de journaux *le kyosk de joornoh*

...post office	...la poste *la post*
...self-service store	...le libre-service *le leebrsehrvees*
...shopping centre	...le centre commercial *le sahηtr komehrsyal*
...stationer's	...la papeterie *la papaytree*
...supermarket	...le supermarché *le sewpehrmarshay*
...sweet shop	...la confiserie *la koηfeezree*
...tobacconist's	...le bureau de tabac *le bewroh de taba*
Have you..., please?	Avez-vous..., s'il vous plaît? *avay voo..., seel voo pleh?*
How much is it?	C'est combien? *seh koηbyaη?*
It's too expensive	C'est trop cher *seh troh shehr*
Haven't you any cheaper?	Vous n'en avez pas de moins cher? *voo nahη avay pah de mwaη shehr?*
I'll take it	Je le prends *je le prahη*
I'll have this one	Je préfère celui-ci *je prayfehr selwee see*
Will you gift-wrap it please?	Voulez-vous me faire un paquet cadeau, s'il vous plaît? *voolay voo m fehr uη pakay kadoh, seel voo pleh?*
Are you open every day?	Vous ouvrez tous les jours? *vooz oovray too lay joor?*

That's all, thank you	C'est tout, merci *seh too mehrsee*
How much do I owe you?	Je vous dois combien? *je voo dwa koŋbyaŋ?*
Here's a 10 euro note	Voilà un billet de dix euros *vwala uŋ beeyeh de deez erroh*
Excuse me, it's not right	Excusez-moi, ce n'est pas juste *ekskewzay mwa, sneh pah jewst*
I owe you...	Je vous dois... *je voo dwa...*
I gave you...	Je vous ai donné... *je vooz ay donay...*
You have to give me three euros change	Il faut me rendre trois euros *eel foh me rahŋdr trwaz erroh*
But you only gave me two back	Mais vous ne m'avez rendu que deux euros *meh voo ne mavay rahŋdew ke derz erroh*

YOU MAY HEAR:

Vous désirez? *voo dayzeeray?*	Can I help you?
Voilà. Et avec ça? *vwala ay avehk sa?*	There you are. Anything else?
Lequel voulez-vous? *lekel voolay voo?*	Which one do you want?
C'est tout? *seh too?*	Is that all?
Ça fait dix euros *sa feh deez erroh*	That's ten euros in all
Et voilà quatre euros que je vous rends *eh vwala katr erroh ke je voo rahŋ*	And there's four euros change

Voulez-vous que je vous fasse un paquet cadeau?
voolay voo ke je voos fas un pakay kadoh?

Shall I gift wrap it?

GENERAL COMPLAINTS

I want to complain about this	Je veux me plaindre de ceci *je ver me plaηdr de sesee*
It's too...	Il est trop... *eel eh troh...*
...dark	...foncé *foηsay*
...expensive	...cher *shehr*
...light (in colour)	...clair *klehr*
...light (in weight)	...léger *layjay*
...narrow/tight	...étroit *aytrwa*
...wide	...large *larj*
This is shop-soiled	Ceci est défraîchi *sesee eh dayfrehshee*
This is broken	Ceci est cassé *sesee eh kussay*
Can you exchange this?	Pouvez-vous l'échanger? *poovay voo layshahnjay?*
I'd like a refund	Je voudrais me faire rembourser *je voodreh me fehr rahηboorsay*
Here's the receipt	Voici le reçu *vwasee le resew*

I bought it yesterday	Je l'ai acheté(e) hier
	je lay ashtay eeyehr
It was a present	C'était un cadeau
	sayteh un kadoh

AT THE DEPARTMENT STORE

Excuse me, where's the department for...?	Excusez-moi, où est le rayon de...?
	ehkskewzay mwa oo eh le rayon de...?
What floor is it on?	C'est à quel étage?
	sehta kel aytaj?
It's on the ground floor	C'est au rez-de-chaussée
	sehtoh ray de shohsay
It's on the first floor	C'est au premier étage
	sehtoh premyehr aytaj
second	deuxième
	derzyehm
third	troisième
	trwazyehm
fourth	quatrième
	katryehm
fifth	cinquième
	sankyehm
Is there a...?	Est-ce qu'il y a...?
	ehskeelya...?
Where is the...?	Où est...?
	oo eh...?
...escalator	...un escalier roulant
	un ehskalyay roolahn
...lift (elevator)	...un ascenseur
	ern asahnserr

...cash desk
...la caisse
la kehs

...staircase
...un escalier
uη ehskalyay

...exit
...la sortie
la sortee

BUYING CLOTHES

Have you...
Avez-vous...
avay voo...

...a bathing suit
...un maillot de bain
uη mayoh de baη

...a blouse
...un chemisier
uη shemeezyay

...a bra
...un soutien-gorge
uη sootyaη gorj

...a cap
...une casquette
ewn kaskeht

...a dress
...une robe
ewn rob

...a handbag
...un sac à main
uη sak a maη

...a hat
...un chapeau
uη shapoh

...some jeans
...un jean
uη jeen

...a jersey
...un tricot
uη treekoh

...a pullover
...un pull
uη pewl

...some pyjamas
...un pyjama
uη peejama

...a raincoat
...un imperméable
ern aηpehrmayabl

...some shoes	...des chaussures
	day shohsewr
...some socks	...des chaussettes
	day shohseht
...some swimming trunks	...un maillot de bain
	uη mayoh de baη
...a T-shirt	...un tee-shirt
	uη tee shert
...some tights	...un collant
	uη kolahη
...some trousers	...un pantalon
	uη pahηtaloη
...some underpants	...un slip
	uη sleep

SIZE

What size are you?	Quelle taille faites vous?
	kehl tahy feht voo?
I take size 12	Je fais du trente-huit
	je feh dew trahηt weet

Men's Suits and Overcoats

British	36	38	40	42	44	46	48	50
American	36	38	40	42	44	46	48	50
Continental	46	48	50/52	54	56	58/60	62	64

Men's Shirts

British	14	$14\frac{1}{2}$	15	$15\frac{1}{2}$	16	$16\frac{1}{2}$	17	$17\frac{1}{2}$
American	14	$14\frac{1}{2}$	15	$15\frac{1}{2}$	16	$16\frac{1}{2}$	17	$17\frac{1}{2}$
Continental	35	36/37	38	39/40	41	42/43	44	45

Men's Shoes

British	7	7½	8	8½	9	9½	10	10½	11
American	7½	8	8½	9	9½	10	10½	11	11½
Continental	41		42		43		44		45

Women's Dresses and Suits

British	8	10	12	14	16	18	20	22
American	-	8	10	12	14	16	18	20
Continental	-	36	38	40	42	44	46	48

Women's Shoes

British	4	4½	5	5½	6	6½	7	7½
American	5½	6	6½	7	7½	8	8½	9
Continental	36	37	38	38	39	40	41	41

I'd like a...dress	Je voudrais une robe…
	je voodreh ewn rob…
...cotton	…en coton
	ahη kotoη
...nylon	…en nylon
	ahη neeloη
...silk	…en soie
	ahη swa
...wool	…en laine
	ahη lehn
...leather	…en cuir
	ahη kweer
...linen	…en lin
	ahη laη

YOU MAY HEAR:

Je peux vous être utile/aider? *je per vooz ehtr ewteelr/ayday?*	Can I help you?
De quelle couleur? *de kehl koolerr?*	What colour?
Le voulez-vous en coton ou en laine? *le voolay voo ahη kotoη oo ahη lehn?*	Do you want it in cotton or wool?
Et avec ça/autre chose? *ay avehk sa/ohtr shohz?*	Anything else?
En voici un à deux cents euros *ahη vwasee uη a der sahη erroh*	Here's one for 200 euros

BUYING FOOD AND DRINK

For other items of food and drink, see **Eating out** section (pages 35–51).

AT THE GROCER'S

a carton of yogurt	un pot de yaourt *uη poh de yaoort*
a litre of milk	un litre de lait *uη leetr de leh*
a kilo of butter	un kilo de beurre *uη keeloh de berr*
six tomatoes	six tomates *see tomat*
two slices of ham	deux tranches de jambon *der trahηsh de jahηboη*
a packet of biscuits	un paquet de biscuits *uη pakay de beeskwee*
a jar of jam	un pot de confiture *uη poh de koηfeetewr*

100 grams of sweets	cent grammes de bonbons
	sahη gram be boηboη
a dozen eggs	une douzaine d'oeufs
	ewn doozehn der

AT THE BAKER'S

a loaf	un pain
	uη paη
a French stick (thick)	une baguette
	ewn bageht
a French stick (thin)	une ficelle
	ewn feesehl
four rolls	quatre petits pains
	katr ptee paη

AT THE FRUITSHOP

a kilo of apples	un kilo de pommes
	uη keeloh de pom
some bananas	des bananes
	day banan
a bunch of grapes	une grappe de raisins
	ewn grap de rehzaη
some oranges	des oranges
	dayz orahηj
half a kilo of peaches	un demi-kilo de pêches
	uη demee keeloh de pehsh
some ripe pears	des poires mûres
	day pwar mewr
some strawberries	des fraises
	day frehz

For vegetables, see *Vegetables, rice and pasta* in the section entitled **Menu guide** (pages 47–8).

AT THE BUTCHER'S

a joint of beef	un rôti de boeuf *un rohtee de berf*
some chicken	du poulet *dew pooleh*
some lamb	de l'agneau *de lanyoh*
two lamb chops	deux côtelettes *der kohtleht*
some liver	du foie *dew fwa*
some veal	du veau *dew voh*

AT THE PORK BUTCHER'S/DELICATESSEN

four rashers of bacon	quatre tranches de lard *katr trahnsh de lar*
three slices of ham	trois tranches de jambon *trwa trahnsh de jahnbon*
300g of cheese	trois cents grammes de fromage *trwa sahn gram de fromaj*
some pork	du porc *dew por*
500g of salami	cinq cents grammes de saucisson *sank sahn gram de sohseeson*
eight sausages	huit saucisses *wee sohsees*

AT THE FISHMONGER'S

a crab	un crabe *un krab*
some cod	de la morue *de la morew*

a herring	un hareng
	uη arahη
a lobster	une langouste/un homard
	ewn lahηgoost/uη omar
some mussels	des moules
	day mool
some oysters	des huîtres
	day weetr
some prawns	des crevettes roses
	day kreveht rohz
some salmon	du saumon
	dew sohmoη
some shrimps	des crevettes grises
	day kreveht greez
a sole	une sole
	ewn sohl
a trout	une truite
	ewn trweet
some tuna	du thon
	dew toη

DRINKS

a bottle of...	une bouteille de...
	ewn bootehy de...
a carton of...	un carton de...
	uη kartoη de...
a can of...	une boîte de...
	ewn bwat de...
apple juice	jus de pommes
	jew de pom
beer	bière
	byehr

Coca-cola	Coca-cola *kohka-kohla*
gin	gin *jeen*
grape juice	jus de raisin *jew de rehsaŋ*
lager	bière blonde *byehr bloŋd*
lemon juice	jus de citron *jew de seetroŋ*
lemonade	limonade *leemonad*
milk	lait *leh*
orange juice	jus d'orange *jew dorahŋj*
red wine	vin rouge *vaŋ rooj*
rosé wine	vin rosé *vaŋ rohzay*
white wine	vin blanc *vaŋ blahŋ*
whisky	un whisky *uŋ weeskee*
brandy	un cognac *uŋ konyak*
port	un porto *uŋ portoh*
rum	un rhum *uŋ rom*
sherry	un xéres *uŋ zeh-res*

vermouth	un vermouth *uη vehrmoot*
vodka	une vodka *ewn vodka*
hot chocolate	un chocolat *uη shokola*
tomato juice	un jus de tomates *uη jew de tomat*
tonic	un Schweppes *uη schwehps*
liqueur	une liqueur *ewn leekerr*
mineral water	l'eau minérale *loh minayral*
fizzy	gazeuse *gazerz*
still	non-gazeuse *noη gazerz*

PHOTOGRAPHY

I'd like a film for this camera	J'aimerais une pellicule pour cet appareil *jehmereh ewn pehleekewl poor seht apareh-y*
black and white	en noir et blanc *ahη nwar ay blahη*
colour	en couleurs *ahη koolerr*
for slides	pour diapositives *poor deeapozeeteev*
24/36 exposures	vingt-quatre/trente-six poses *vaη katr/trahηt see pohz*

How much do you charge for developing?	Combien coûte le développement? *koηbyan koot le dayvlopmahη?*
I want....prints of this photo	Je voudrais...copies de cette photo *je voodreh...kopee de seht fotoh*
matt/glossy finish	sur papier mat/brillant *sewr papyay mat/breeyahη*
When will the photos be ready?	Quand est-ce que les photos seront prêtes? *kahηtehske lay fotoh seroη preht?*
I need batteries for this camera	Il me faut des piles pour cet appareil *eel me foh day peel poor seht apareh-y*
Can you repair this camera?	Pouvez-vous réparer cet appareil? *poovay voo rayparay seht apareh-y?*
The film/wind-on mechanism is jammed	Le film/le levier d'avancement est bloqué *le feelm/le levyay davaηhsmahη eh blokay*

SERVICES

Write to *l'Office de Tourisme* in the city you plan to visit, or to the
Syndicat d'Initiative (information bureau) in smaller towns. These
will give you plenty of brochures and information about specialised
holidays, local tour operators, travel agents, etc. Get the address
from a good holiday guide, or try a letter using the name of the city
as the address. An international reply coupon will be appreciated.

VISITING A TOWN

Where is...?	Où se trouve...? *oo se troov...?*
...the tourist information office	...le Syndicat d'Initiative *le saŋdeeka deeneesyateev*
...the castle	...le château *le shahtoh*
...the cathedral	...la cathédrale *la kataydral*
...the market	...le marché *le marshay*
...the museum	...le musée *le mewzay*
...the palace	...le palais *le paleh*
...the shopping centre	...le centre commercial *le sahŋtr komehrsyal*
Is it open on Sundays?	C'est ouvert le dimanche? *seht oovehr le deemahŋsh?*
Can I take photos?	Il est permis de prendre des photos? *eel eh perhrmee de prahŋdr day fotoh?*

Do you have a guidebook in English?	Avez-vous un guide en anglais?
	avay voo uη geed ahn ahηgleh?
Is there a guided tour?	Y a-t-il une visite guidée?
	yateel ewn veezeet geeday?
Do you have any postcards?	Avez-vous des cartes postales?
	avay voo day kart postal?

INFORMATION

Where's the information bureau?	Où se trouve le syndicat d'initiative?
	oo se troov le saηdeeka deeneesyateev?
I should like some information about...	Je voudrais me renseigner sur...
	je voodreh me rahηsehnyay sewr...
...boarding houses	...les pensions
	lay pahηsyoη
...campsites	...les campings
	lay kahηpeeng
...castles	...les châteaux
	lay shahtoh
...excursions	...les excursions
	layz ehxkewrzyoη
...exhibitions	...les expositions
	layz ehxpozeesyoη
...evening amusements	...les divertissements dans la soirée
	lay deevehrteesmahη dahη la swaray
...hotels	...les hôtels
	layz ohtehl
...monuments	...les monuments historiques
	lay monewmahη eestoreek

...museums	...les musées *lay mewzay*
...shows	...les spectacles *lay spehktakl*
...sports facilities	...les équipements sportifs *layz aykeepmahη sporteef*
Have you...	Avez-vous... *avay voo...*
...some brochures	...quelques brochures *kehlke broshewr*
...some leaflets	...quelques dépliants *kehlke daypleeahη*
...a list of hotels	...une liste des hôtels *ewn leest dayz ohtehl*
...a map of the town	...une carte de la ville *ewn kart de la veel*
...a town plan	...un plan de la ville *uη plahη de la veel*
Can one/we/you...?	Est-ce qu'on peut...? *ehskoη per...?*
...hire...	...louer... *looay...*
...visit...	...visiter... *veezeetay...*
...go there every day	...y aller tous les jours *ee alay too lay joor*

USEFUL QUESTIONS

Where is...?	Où se trouve...? *oo se troov...?*
When does it begin?	Ça commence à quelle heure? *sa komahηs a kehl err?*

When does it end?	Ça finit à quelle heure? *sa feenee a kehl err?*
How much does it cost?	Ça coûte combien? *sa koot koŋbyaŋ?*
What's the price of...?	Quel est le prix de...? *kehl eh le pree de...?*

CLEANING AND REPAIRS

Dry cleaning prices are relatively expensive, and the time taken may be 24 hours.

I'm looking for...	Je cherche... *je shehrsh*
...a dry cleaner's	...une teinturerie *ewn taŋtewreree*
...an electrician	...un électricien *uŋ aylehktreesyaŋ*
...a garage mechanic	...un garagiste *uŋ garajeest*
...a laundrette	...une laverie automatique *ewn lavree otomateek*
...a plumber	...un plombier *uŋ plohŋbyay*
...a repair shop	...un atelier de réparations *uŋ atelyay de rayparasyoŋ*
...a shoe repairer	...un cordonnier *uŋ kordonyay*
It's not working	Ça ne marche pas *sa ne marsh pah*
It has broken down	Il (elle) est en panne *eel (ehl) eht ahŋ pan*
It's torn	Il (elle) est déchiré(e) *eel (ehl) eh daysheeray*

Can you repair my watch?

Est-ce que vous pouvez réparer
ma montre?
*ehske voo poovay rayparay ma
moηtr?*

How much is it to dry clean
my sweater?

C'est combien pour nettoyer mon
tricot à sec?
*seh koηbyaη poor nehtwayay
moη treekoh a sehk ?*

It needs heeling

Il est éculé
eel eht aykewlay

to heel a shoe

remettre un talon
remehtr uη taloη

to put a sole on a shoe

ressemeler un soulier
resemlay uη soolyay

AT THE LAUNDERETTE

How long will you take to wash
the clothes?

Vous allez mettre combien de
temps à laver les vêtements?
*vooz alay mehtr koηbyaη de
tahη a lavay lay vehtmahη?*

When will it be ready?

Quand est-ce qu'il sera prêt?
kahηt ehskeel sera preh?

How long will it take?

Ça va demander combien
de temps?
*sa va demahηday koηbyaη
de tahη?*

Will it be long?

On en a pour longtemps?
on ahn a poor loηtahη?

AT THE DIY STORE

I need a...

Il me faut...
eel me foh

...bicycle pump

...une pompe
   ewn pohηp

...fuse	...un plomb/un fusible *uη plohη/uη fewzeebl*
...needle	...une aiguille *ewn aygweey*
...thread	...un fil *uη feel*
...repair kit	...une trousse de réparation *ewn troos de reyparasyoη*
...screwdriver	...un tournevis *uη toornevees*
It's fused	Il y a un plomb de sauté *eelya uη plohη de sohtay*

BANKS AND POST OFFICES
AT THE BANK OR EXCHANGE BUREAU

BUSINESS HOURS
Banks are usually open from 9 am till noon and from 2 to 4 pm on weekdays. They are usually closed either Saturdays or Mondays. Sometimes the smaller branches close for lunch. Exchange bureaux are often open later. You should have your passport at hand when cashing a traveller's cheque.

I'm looking for an exchange bureau?	Je cherche un bureau de change *je shersh uη bewroh de shahnj*
I'd like to cash...	Je voudrais encaisser... *je voodreh eηcaysay...*
...a traveller's cheque	...un chèque de voyage *uη shehk de vwayaj*
...two cheques of 100 euros	...deux chèques de cent euros *der shehk de sahη erroh*
I'd like to change some pounds	Je voudrais changer des livres *je voodreh shahηjay day leevr*
What is the rate of exchange?	Quel est le taux du change? *kehl eh le toh dew shahηj?*
Please give me...	Donnez-moi...s'il vous plaît *donaymwa...seel voo pleh*
...notes	...des billets *day beeyay*
...small change	...de la monnaie *de la moneh*
Here is my passport	Voici mon passeport *vwasee moη paspor*
Here it is	Le voici *le vwasee*

Is it free?	C'est gratuit?
	seh gratwee?
Is it included?	C'est compris?
	seh koηpree?

YOU MAY HEAR:

Vous avez votre passeport?	Have you got your passport?
vooz avay votr paspor?	
Vous voulez combien?	How much do you want?
voo voolay koηbyaη?	
Voulez-vous signer ici?	Will you sign here?
voolay voo seenyay eesee?	
Passez à la caisse	You must go to the cash desk
pasay a la kehs	

in large notes	en grosses coupures
	ahη grohs koopewr
in small notes	en petites coupures
	ahη pteet koopewr
account	le compte
	le koηt
balance	le solde
	le sold
breakdown/detailed account	le décompte
	le daykoηt
cheque (personal)	le chèque
	le shehk
cheque book	le carnet de chèques
	le karnay de shehk
commission	la commission
	la komeesyoη
cash card	la carte bleue
	la kart bler

credit card	la carte de crédit *la karte de kraydee*
visa card	la carte visa *la kart veeza*
equivalent value	la contrevaleur *la kontrevalerr*
Eurocheques	des eurochèques *days errohshehk*
extra charge	le supplément *le sewplaymahn*
foreign currency	des devises étrangères *day deveez aytrahnjehr*
form	le bon/la fiche *le bon/la feesh*
mistake	une erreur *ewn ehrerr*
receipt	le reçu *le resew*
reduction	la réduction *la raydewksyon*
telex	le télex *le taylehx*
total	le montant *le montahn*
transfer	le virement *le veermahn*
to make a credit transfer	faire un virement *fehr un veermahn*
traveller's cheque	le chèque de voyage *le shehk de vwayaj*

BUSINESS EXPRESSIONS

I'm	Je suis *jswee…*
…Mr Smith	…Monsieur Smith *msyer smeeth*
…Mrs Smith	…Madame Smith *madam smeeth*
…Miss Smith	…Mademoiselle Smith *mamwazehl smeeth*
I'm from…(company)	Je représente la compagnie… *je reprayzahη la koηpanyee…*
I have an appointment with…	J'ai un rendez-vous avec… *jay uη rahηday voo avehk…*
Could I speak to…	Est-ce que je peux parler avec… *ehske je per parlay avehk*
…the sales manager	…le directeur commercial *le deerehkterr komehrsyal*
…the personnel manager	…le chef du personnel *le shehf dew pehrsonehl*
Here is my card	Voici ma carte *vwasee ma kart*
I'm sorry I'm late	Je suis désolé(e), je suis en retard *jswee dayzolay, jswee ahη retar*
I'm in the hotel	Je suis à l'hôtel… *jswee a lohtehl*
Please ask him to call me	Voulez-vous lui demander de m'appeler? *voolay voo lwee demahηday de maplay?*

AT THE POST OFFICE

BUSINESS HOURS

Most post offices are open from 8 am to 7 pm on weekdays (often closed 12 noon – 2 pm) and from 8 am to noon on Saturdays.

The main post office at 52 rue du Louvre 75001 Paris is open 24 hours daily. Letters can be sent *poste restante* to any French post office.

Post offices are recognisable by *La Poste* signs in France, by the PTT signs in Switzerland and by *Postel/Posterijen* in Belgium.

I'm looking for...	Je cherche... *je shehrsh*
...the post office	...la poste *la post*
...a letter box (mailbox)	...une boîte aux lettres *ewn bwat oh letr*
...a phone booth	...une cabine téléphonique *ewn kabeen taylayfoneek*
How much is it to send...?	C'est combien pour envoyer...? *seh koηbyaη poor ahηvwayay...?*
I'd like to send...	Je voudrais envoyer... *je voodreh ahηvwayay...*
...a letter	...une lettre *ewn lehtr*
...a parcel	...un colis *uη kolee*
...a postcard	...une carte-postale *ewn kartpostal*

You cannot make telephone calls or send telegrams from Belgian Post Offices; for this you have to look for a special *Téléphone/Télégraphe* office.

...a postal order	...un mandat postal *uη mahηda postal*
...to Britain	...en Grande-Bretagne *ahη grahηd bretanye*
...to Ireland	...en Irlande *ahn eerlahηd*
...to the USA	...aux Etats-Unis *ohz aytaz ewnee*
...to Australia	...en Australie *ahn ostralee*
I would like...	Je voudrais... *je voodreh...*
...three 1 euro stamps	...trois timbres à un euro *trwa taηbr a uη erroh*
...two 50-centime stamps	...deux timbres à cinquante centimes *der taηbr a saηkahηt sahηteem*
...one 2-euro stamp	...un timbre à deux euros *uη taηbr a derz erroh*
Which counter?	Quel guichet? *kehl geeshay?*
I'd like a phonecard	Je voudrais une Télécarte *je voodreh ewn taylaykart*
Can you give me the directory, please	Pouvez-vous me donner l'annuaire, s'il vous plaît? *poovay voo me donay lanewehr, seel voo pleh?*

YOU MAY HEAR:

Voilà. C'est tout? *vwala seh too?*	There you are. Is that all?
Il faut remplir cette fiche *eel foh rahηpleer seht feesh*	You have to fill out this form

Qu'est-ce qu'il y a dedans?
kehskeelya dedahη?

What's inside?

C'est trop lourd
seh troh loor

It's too heavy

TELEPHONING

Special 'telephone offices' are available in major post offices, where the calls are controlled by operators whom you pay when the call has finished. At 52 rue du Louvre, Paris, you can find telephone directories for all countries.

Street phone boxes are often vandalised and unusable, so it may be quicker to find a post office. Theoretically, unused coins are returned, but as the mechanism is not always working correctly, it is sensible to use the smallest denomination possible. Phone boxes are available to take coins and phone cards *(cartes téléphoniques)*. Phone cards can be bought at a *bureau de tabac*.

There are still phones in cafés, restaurants and post offices using tokens *(jetons)* which you can buy at the counter.

It is wise to ask the rates if you are phoning abroad from a hotel or restaurant, as they are allowed to charge higher prices than normal rates.

To give you the phone number 123 12 34, a French person would normally express the number as 'one hundred and twenty three, twelve, thirty-four', so if you wish to be given the number in the English way, ask for the number *chiffre par chiffre*.

When phoning from the UK to France use the access code **0033**, then the French number minus the first zero. For example, the French number 01 41 56 78 00 becomes 0033 1 41 56 78 00. When phoning from France to the UK use the access code **0044**, then the English number minus the first zero.
Useful website: www.pagesjaunes.com

Cheap rates:
50% extra time: weekdays between 7 pm and 8 am and weekends starting 2 pm on Saturdays.

Phone cards
Télécartes may be obtained from post offices, tobacconists and newsagents.

Useful numbers
Operator 13, Directory Enquiries 12.

Hello!	Allô!
	aloh!
Can you help me, please?	Pouvez-vous m'aider, s'il vous plaît?
	poovay voo mehday seel voo pleh?
I'd like the international operator	Je voudrais le service international
	je voodreh le sehrvees aɳtehrnasyonal
Directory Enquiries, please	Renseignements, s'il vous plaît
	rahɳsehnymahɳ, seel voo pleh
What's the dialling code for Britain?	Quel est l'indicatif de la Grande-Bretagne?
	kehl eh laɳdeekateef de la grahɳd bretanye

I want extension...please	Je voudrais le poste...s'il vous plaît *je voodreh le post...seel voo pleh*
Is...there, please?	Est-ce que...est là, s'il vous plaît? *ehske...eh la, seel voo pleh?*
It's...speaking	C'est...à l'appareil *seh...a lapareh-y*
I'd like to reverse the charges	Je voudrais téléphoner en PCV *je voodreh taylayfonay ahη pay say vay*
I'm telephoning to tell you my arrival time	Je téléphone pour te dire l'heure de mon arrivée *je taylayfon poor te deer lerr de moη areevay*
I'm expecting to arrive...	Je compte arriver... *je kohηt areevay...*
...tomorrow	...demain *demaη*
...at...o'clock	...à...heures *a...err*
...this afternoon	...cet après-midi *seht apreh meedee*
...before six o'clock	avant six heures *avahη seez err*
...next week	...la semaine prochaine *la smehn proshehn*

YOU MAY SEE:

décrocher le combiné	lift the receiver
la fente	the slot
composer le numéro	dial the number

| la tonalité | the dialling tone |
| raccrocher | to hang up |

YOU MAY HEAR:

Quel numéro demandez-vous? *kehl newmayroh demahηdayvoo?*	What number are you calling?
Ce n'est pas libre *se neh pah leebr*	The line's engaged
C'est de la part de qui? *seh de la par de kee?*	Who's speaking?
Il n'y a personne *eel nya pehrson*	There's no answer
Ne quittez pas *ne keetay pah*	Hold the line
à l'appareil *a lapareh-y*	speaking
en dérangement/en panne *ahη dayrahηjmahη/ahη pan*	out of order
Combien d'unités? *koηbyaη dewneetay?*	How many units (phonecard)?
avec préavis *avehk prayavee*	person-to-person
PCV *pay say vay*	reverse charge call
Vous vous êtes trompé(e) de numéro *voo voozeht troηpay de newmayroh*	You've got a wrong number

EMERGENCIES

The British Consulate should be used only as a last resort. Police, insurance companies, etc. should be contacted first. Make a separate list of credit card numbers and passport numbers, and keep a note of emergency telephone numbers in case of theft.

British Consulates
A useful website is: www.amb-grandebretagne.fr

Telephone numbers:

Paris: Consulate 01 44 51 31 02
                               Embassy 01 44 51 31 00
                               (01 becomes 0033 1 if
                               phoning from the UK)

Bordeaux:	05 57 22 21 (05 becomes 0033 5)	
Lille:	03 20 12 82 72 (03 becomes 0033 3)	
Lyon:	04 72 77 81 70 (04 becomes 0033 4)	
Marseille:	04 91 15 72 10 (04 becomes 0033 4)	

Emergency telephone numbers

	France	Belgium	Switzerland
Fire	18	100*	118
Ambulance	15(SAMU)	100*	144
Police	17	101*	117

*or dial 112 and ask for the service you need.

ROAD ACCIDENTS

In case of minor accident in France, it is usually sufficient to fill in a standard accident form *(un constat)*. Each driver signs the other's copy.

My insurance company	Ma compagnie d'assurances *ma koηpanyee dasewrahηs*
is called...	s'appelle... *sapehl*
Here's...	Voici... *vwasee*
...my insurance certificate	...ma carte d'assurance *ma kart dasewrahηs*
...my insurance policy	...ma police d'assurance *ma polees dasewrahηs*
Where is...?	Où se trouve...? *oo se troov...?*

If you cannot read French and don't know what you are signing, it is safer to call the police (*la police, les gendarmes*): you must always do this in the case of a major accident.

...the police station	...le poste de police *le post de polees* ...le commissariat *le komeesareeya* ...la gendarmerie *la jahηdarmeree*
...the hospital	...l'hôpital *lohpeetal*
I must telephone	Je dois téléphoner *je dwa taylayfonay*
There has been...	Il y a eu... *Eelya ew*
...an accident	...un accident *uη akseedahη*
...a fire	...un feu *uη fer*

A CAR BREAKDOWN

Please refer to *A car breakdown* in the section on **Driving** (pages 83–5).

YOU MAY HEAR:

Vous avez attrapé une contravention *vooz avay atrapay ewn koηtravahηsyoη*	You have got a fine
Vous avez excédé la limitation de vitesse *vooz avay ehksayday la leemeetasyoη de veetehs*	You have exceeded the speed limit

Quel est votre numéro d'immatriculation? *kehl eh votre newmayroh deematreekewlasyoη?*	What is your registration number?
Voiture immatriculée XFV 425 G *vwatewr eematreekewlay eex ehf vay katre sahη vaηsaηk jay*	Car with registration no. XFV 425 G
Où est votre...? *oo eh votr...?*	Where is your...?
...permis de conduire *pehrmee de koηdweer*	...driving licence
...carte d'immatriculation *kart deematreekewlasyoη*	...registration certificate
...carte verte *kart vehrt*	...Green card
...carte d'assurance *kart dassewrahηs*	...certificate of insurance
...plaque de nationalité *plak de nasyonaleetay*	...nationality plate
Vous avez une pièce d'identité? *vooz avay ewn pyehs deedahη teetay?*	Have you some identification?
Est-ce que les feux étaient rouges? *ehske lay fer ayteh rooj?*	Were the lights red?

USEFUL VOCABULARY

(snow) chains	les chaînes *lay shehn*
a fine	une contravention *ewn koηtravahηsyoη*
	une amende *ewn amahηd*

passengers	les passagers *lay passajay*
at the back	à l'arrière *a laryehr*
traffic lights	les feux *lay fer*
dipped headlights	les feux de croisement *lay fer de krwazmahη*
green light	le feu vert *le fer vehr*
red light	le feu rouge *le fer rooj*
rear lights	les feux arrière *lay fer aryehr*
side lights	les feux de position *lay fer de pozeesyoη*
warning light	le voyant *le vwayahη*
warning sign	le panneau avertisseur *le panoh avehrteeserr*
to brake	freiner *frehnay*
to cross	traverser *travehrsay*
to collide with	entrer en collision avec *ahηtray ahη koleezyoη avehk*
to have priority	avoir la priorité *avwar la preeoritay*
to switch on (lights)	allumer *alewmay*
to switch off (lights)	éteindre *aytaηdre*

to hurt	blesser *blehsay*
to knock down	renverser/écraser *rahɲvehrsay/aykrazay*
to overtake	dépasser *daypasay*
to stop	s'arrêter *sarehtay*
I was careful	J'ai fait attention *jay feht atahɲsyoɲ*
I was careless	Je n'ai pas fait attention *jnay pah feht atahɲsyoɲ*
He was careless	Il n'a pas fait attention *eel na pah feht atahɲsyoɲ*
I've phoned	J'ai téléphoné *jay taylayfonay*
I'm cold	J'ai froid *jay frwa*
I'm hungry	J'ai faim *jay faɲ*
I'm thirsty	J'ai soif *jay swaf*
Are you hurt?	Etes-vous blessé(e)? *eht voo blehsay?*
Be careful!	Attention! *atahɲsyoɲ!*
I didn't know that...	Je ne savais pas que... *je ne saveh pah ke...*
you must	il faut *eel foh*
you must not	il ne faut pas *eel ne foh pah*

LOST PROPERTY

Lost jewellery, camera, clothing, luggage: you should report to the nearest police station, where you will have to describe the lost item in French. Ask for a copy of this report if you are claiming for the loss with an insurance company. You can also try the local lost property office.

Lost credit cards: should be reported immediately to your bank according to the instructions given on issue, and also to the police.

Where's the lost property office?	Où se trouve le bureau des objets trouvés? *oo se troov le bewroh dayz objay troovay?*
I've lost...	J'ai perdu... *jay pehrdew*
...my handbag	...mon sac à main *mon sak a man*
...my money	...mon argent *mon arjahn*
...my passport	...mon passeport *mon paspor*
...my suitcase	...ma valise *ma valeez*
...my wallet	...mon portefeuille *mon portfe-y*
...my umbrella	...mon parapluie *mon paraplwee*
...my ring	...ma bague *ma bag*
I lost it...	je l'ai perdu... *je lay pehrdew...*
...this morning	...ce matin *se matan*

...today	...aujourd'hui *ohjoordwee*
...yesterday	...hier *ee-ehr*
...3 days ago	...il y a trois jours *eelya trwa joor*
My name's on it	Mon nom est marqué dessus *moη noη eh markay desew*
It is...	Il (elle) est... *eel (ehl) eh...*
...black	...noir *nwar*
...dark blue	...bleu foncé *bler foηsay*
...light blue	...bleu clair *bler klehr*
...empty	...vide *veed*
...full	...plein *plaη*
...green	...vert *vehr*
...(quite) large	...(assez) grand *asay grahη*
...long	...long *loη*
...narrow	...étroit *aytrwa*
...new	...neuf *nerf*
...rectangular	...rectangulaire *rehktahηgewlehr*

...red | ...rouge
| *rooj*

...round | ...rond
| *ron*

...short | ...court
| *koor*

...square | ...carré
| *karay*

...white | ...blanc
| *blahn*

...wide | ...large
| *larj*

...yellow | ...jaune
| *john*

...made of gold | ...en or
| *ahn or*

...made of leather | ...en cuir
| *ahn kweer*

...made of metal | ...en métal
| *ahn maytal*

...made of nylon | ...en nylon
| *ahn neelon*

...made of plastic | ...en plastique
| *ahn plasteek*

...made of silver | ...en argent
| *ahn arjahn*

...made of wood | ...en bois
| *ahn bwa*

YOU MAY HEAR:

Je peux vous aider?
je per vooz ayday?

Can I help you?

Quand est-ce que vous l'avez
perdu?
kahη tehske voo lavay pehrdew?

When did you lose it?

Qu'est-ce qu'il y avait dedans?
kehskeelyaveh dedahη?

What was there inside?

Il (elle) est comment?
eel (ehl) eh komahη?

What's it like?

Revenez demain, ou téléphonez
revenay demaη oo taylayfonay

Come back tomorrow, or phone

DICTIONARY

All nouns preceded by *le* or *un* are masculine; *la* or *une* denote
feminine nouns. Nouns are identified as either masculine (m) or
feminine (f) where this is not otherwise clear. Both masculine and feminine
forms are given for adjectives e.g. hot: chaud(e) = chaud (m)/chaude (f).

A
abbey une abbaye
to be able pouvoir
about/roughly environ
above au-dessus (de)/en haut
abroad à l'étranger
abscess un abcès
absent absent(e)
to accept accepter
accident un accident
account le compte
accurate exact(e)/correct(e)
ache une douleur
in addition en plus
address une adresse
admission l'entrée (f)
to admit laisser entrer
adult un(e) adulte
in avance en avance
advertisement une annonce
aeroplane un avion
after après/au bout de
afternoon un après-midi
afternoon performance la matinée
aftershave (lotion) une lotion
 après-rasage
again encore/de nouveau
age un âge
agency une agence
air l'air (m)
 by air par avion
 open air en plein air
air bed le matelas pneumatique
air conditioned climatisé(e)/air
 conditionné(e)
airmail par avion
airport un aéroport
air sickness le mal de l'air
air terminal un aérogare
all/every tout(e)
all year toute l'année
allergy une allergie

allowed permis(e)
also aussi
always toujours
amazing incroyable
ambulance une ambulance
America l'Amérique (f)
American américain(e)
amount (money) la quantité/la somme
amusements les divertissements (m)
amusing amusant(e)/drôle
anchovies les anchois (m)
animal un animal
ankle la cheville
anorak un anorak
antibiotic un antibiotique
antiques les antiquités (f)
antiseptic antiseptique
anything quelque chose/n'importe quoi
appetizing appétissant(e)
apple la pomme
apple juice le jus de pommes
appliance un appareil
appointment le rendez-vous
approximately à peu pres
apricot un abricot
April avril
architect un architecte
area (part of town) un quartier
area (part of country) une région
around autour (de)
 all around tout autour
arrival une arrivée
to arrive arriver
art art (m)
art gallery une galerie d'art
article/item un article
as/like comme
ashtray le cendrier
to ask (for) demander
asparagus les asperges (f)
aspirin l'aspirine (f)
assistant un employé

asthma l'asthme (m)
athletics l'athlétisme (m)
attack/fit la crise
attendant attendant
  petrol attendant le pompiste
August août
automatic automatique
average moyen(ne)
away /a long way away loin
  go away! allez-vous en!
awful affreux(-euse)/moche/terrible

B
baby le bébé
baby food les aliments (m) pour bébés
bachelor le célibataire
back le dos
  at the back à l'arrière
backache le mal de reins
bacon le lard
bacon and eggs les oeufs (m) au bacon
bad mauvais(e)
badly mal
bag le sac
baggage/bags les bagages (m)
baked au four
baker's la boulangerie
balance (money) le solde
balcony le balcon
ball (toy) le ballon
ball (dance) la balle
ballet le ballet
ball-point pen le stylo (à bille)
banana la banane
bandage le pansement
bank la banque
bank note le billet de banque
bar le bar
Barclaycard/Visa la carte bleue
barmaid la serveuse
barrier (automatic) le portillon
  automatique
bath le bain/la baignoire
to have a bath prendre un bain
to bathe se baigner
bathroom la salle de bains
battery (car) la batterie
to be être/se trouver
beach la plage

bean le haricot
  green beans les haricots verts
beard la barbe
beautiful beau (belle)
because parce que/car
bed le lit
bed and breakfast chambre avec
  petit déjeuner
bedroom la chambre
bee une abeille
beef le boeuf/le rosbif
beer la bière
beetroot la betterave
before (time) avant
before (place) devant
to begin commencer
beginning le début
behind derrière/en arrière
Belgian belge
Belgium Belgique
bell (church) la cloche
bell (electric) la sonnette
below en bas
belt la ceinture
  safety belt la ceinture de sécurité
bend (in road) le virage
beret le béret
beside à côté de
better meilleur
bicycle le vélo/la bicyclette
  by bicycle en vélo
bicycle pump la pompe
bidet le bidet
big (fat) gros(se)
big (tall) grand(e)
bill la note/l'addition (f)
bindings les fixations (f)
bird un oiseau
biro le stylo
birthdate la date de naissance
birthday un anniversaire
  happy birthday! bon anniversaire!
biscuit le biscuit
black noir(e)
blanket la couverture
block (of flats) un immeuble
blood le sang
  (high blood pressure la tension
  (élevée)

blouse le chemisier
blown (fuse/light/bulb) sauté(e)
blue bleu(e)
board
  full board la pension complète
  half board la demi-pension
boarding house la pension
boat le bateau
  by boat en bateau/par le bateau
body le corps
boiled (potatoes) nature, vapeur
bomber jacket le blouson
to book/reserve réserver/retenir
book le livre
booking/reservation la réservation
booklet le carnet
boot (of car) le coffre
boot (footwear) la botte
boring ennuyeux (-euse)
to borrow emprunter
boss le patron/la patronne
bottle la bouteille
bottom (far end) le fond
boulevard le boulevard
bowl le bol
box la boîte
boxing la boxe
boy le garçon
bra le soutien-gorge
brake le frein
brave/courageous courageux (-euse)
bread le pain/la baguette
to break casser
to break down être en panne/tomber
  en panne
breakdown (mechanical) la panne
breakfast le petit déjeuner
bridge le pont
briefs/pants le slip/la culotte
to bring apporter
Britain la Grande-Bretagne
British britannique
Brittany la Bretagne
broadcast/programme une émission
broken down/not working en panne
brother le frère
brown brun/marron
brush la brosse
Brussels Bruxelles

buffet le buffet
building le bâtiment
bulb une ampoule
to burgle cambrioler
burnt brûlé(e)
burst (tyre) crevé(e)
bus un autobus/un bus
  by bus en bus/en autobus
bus station la gare routière
bus stop un arrêt
butcher's la boucherie
  pork butcher's la charcuterie
butter le beurre
button le bouton
to buy acheter

C
cabbage le chou
cake le gâteau
cake shop la pâtisserie
calculator le calculateur de poche
calf le veau
to call appeler
to call back rappeler
  to make a reverse-charge call
  téléphoner en PCV
call (on phone) le coup de téléphone
calm calme
calor gas le butane
calor gas store le dépôt de butane
camera un appareil (photo)
to camp camper
camp bed le lit de camp
camper le campeur
camping equipment le matériel de
  camping
campsite le camping/le terrain
  de camping
can la boîte
Canada le Canada
  in/to Canada au Canada
Canadian canadien(enne)
to cancel annuler
canteen la cantine
car une auto/une voiture
car hire la location de voitures
car hire agency l'agence (f) de location
  de voitures
car sickness le mal de la route

I am car sick je suis malade en voiture
carafe la carafe
caravan la caravane
card la carte
 banker's card la carte bancaire
 credit card la carte de crédit
 to play cards jouer aux cartes
to be careful faire attention
 be careful! Attention!
caretaker le/la concierge
carriage la voiture
to carry/wear porter
carton (of cigarettes) la cartouche
 (of yoghurt) le pot
 (of milk) le carton
cartoon le dessin animé
case la valise
cash l'argent (m)/le liquide
to cash a cheque toucher/encaisser un
 chèque
cashdesk la caisse
cassette la cassette
 cassette recorder le magnétophone
castle le château
cathedral la cathédrale
Catholic catholique
cauliflower le chou-fleur
cellar la cave
centime le centime
centimetre le centimètre
centre le centre
 town centre le centre-ville
 shopping centre le centre commercial
certain certain(e)
certainly certainement
chain la chaîne
chair la chaise
to change changer
change la monnaie
channel (on TV) la chaîne
(English) Channel la Manche
charge le prix/le tarif
 extra charge le supplément
cheap bon marché
cheaper moins cher(chère)
to check vérifier
check-out la caisse
cheese le fromage
chemist's la pharmacie
cheque le chèque

traveller's cheque le chèque de voyage
cheque book le carnet de chèques
cherry la cerise
chewing gum le chewing-gum
chicken le poulet
child un(e) enfant
chips les frites (f)
chocolate le chocolat
 bar of chocolate la plaque de chocolat
choice le choix
to choose choisir
chop la côtelette
Christmas Noël (m)
church une église
cider le cidre
cigarette la cigarette
 cigarette case un étui à cigarettes
cine-camera la caméra
cinema le cinéma
circle (in theatre) le balcon
class la classe
 first class première classe
 second class seconde classe
to clean nettoyer
 to have something cleaned faire
 nettoyer
clean propre
cliff la falaise
climbing/mountaineering l'alpinisme (m)
clinic la clinique
clock une horloge
to close fermer
 closed fermé(e)
cloth (fabric) le tissu
cloth (duster) le torchon
clothes les vêtements (m)
 sports clothes le tenue de sport
club le club
 youth club la maison des jeunes
clutch un embrayage
coach (railway) le wagon/la voiture
coach (bus) un car
 by coach en car
coast la côte
coat le manteau
Coca-Cola le Coca-Cola
cod le cabillaud/la morue
coeducational mixte
coffee le café
 (white) café au lait

DICTIONARY

(with cream) café-crème
(black) café nature
coffee pot la cafetière
coin la pièce
cold froid(e)
  to have a cold avoir un rhume/être
  enrhumé(e)
  I am cold j'ai froid
collection la collection
  (of post) la levée
collision la collision
colour la couleur
to come venir
comedy (film) un film comique
comfortable confortable
commission la commission
compact disc le disque compact
compartement le compartiment
to complain faire une réclamation/se
  plaindre
  complaint la réclamation
complete complet(-ète)
compulsory obligatoire
computer le calculateur/l'ordinateur
computer games les jeux d'ordinateur
concert le concert
confectioner's la confiserie
congratulations! Félicitations!
connection (in Metro)
  la correspondance
constipated constipé(e)
consulate le consulat
consulting room la salle de
  consultation
convenient commode
to cook faire la cuisine
cook le chef
cooked cuit(e)
  well cooked bien cuit(e)
cooker la cuisinière
corkscrew le tire-bouchon
corn (food) le maïs
corn (on foot) le cor
corner le coin
correct exact/correct
corridor le corridor
to cost coûter
  cost le prix/le tarif
costume le costume
  bathing costume le maillot de bain

cotton le coton
  made of cotton en coton
cotton wool le coton hydrophile/l'ouate
couchette la couchette
to cough tousser
cough drops les pastilles (f) contre
  la toux
council flat un HLM
counter le guichet
counter (in shop) le rayon/le comptoir
country le pays
countryside la campagne
course le cours
rover charge le couvert
crab le crabe
crayfish les écrevisses (f)
cream la crème
credit le crédit
  credit card la carte de crédit
cricket le cricket
crisps les chips (f)
cross la croix
  level crossing le passage à niveau
  pedestrian crossing le passage (pour
  piétons)
  sea crossing la traversée
crossroads le carrefour
cup la tasse
currency
  (foreign) les devises étrangères (f)
customs la douane
customs duty la taxe/les droits de
  douane
to cut couper
cyclist le/la cycliste

D
daily quotidien(ne)
dairy la crémerie
to dance danser
dance le bal
danger le danger
dangerous dangereux (-euse)
dark (of colour) foncé(e)
dark (of sky) noir(e)
date la date
daughter la fille
day le jour/la journée
  the day before la veille, avant-hier
  the next day le lendemain

the day after tomorrow après-demain
dead mort(e)
to deal with s'occuper de
December décembre
deck chair la chaise longue/le transat
to declare déclarer
  nothing to declare rien à déclarer
deep profond(e)
delay le retard
  delayed en retard
delicatessen la charcuterie
dentist le/la dentiste
deodorant le déodorant
department le département/le rayon
departure gate la porte de départ
departure lounge la salle de départ
departure time l'heure de départ
to depend dépendre
  that depends ça dépend
deposit la caution
desk (= cashdesk) la caisse
dessert le dessert
destination la destination
diabetic diabétique
to dial composer le numéro
  to dial 999 appeler police-secours
dialling code l'indicatif (m)
dialling tone la tonalité
diarrhoea la diarrhée/la colique
diesel (oil) le gas-oil
to dine dîner
dining room la salle à manger
diploma le brevet/le certificat/le
  diplôme
direction le sens/la direction
  all directions toutes directions
directory un annuaire
dirty sale
disco la disco(thèque)
  to go to a disco aller en boîte
dish le plat
distance la distance
distant/far away loin/éloigné(e)
diversion la déviation
divorced divorcé(e)
dizzy spells des vertiges (m)
to do faire
doctor le docteur/le médecin
documentary le documentaire
dog le chien

door la porte
  (of car) la portière
dormitory le dortoir
doubt la doute
  no doubt sans doute
dozen la douzaine
Dover Douvres
drawing le dessin
dress la robe
to drink boire
drink la boisson
drinkable (of water) potable
  (non-)drinking water eau (non) potable
to drive conduire/rouler
  drive la randonnée
driver le chauffeur/le conducteur
drunk ivre
to dry clean nettoyer à sec
dry cleaning/dry cleaner's le nettoyage
  à sec
dubbed doublé(e)
dubbed in French en version française
duration la durée
dust la poussière
dustbin la poubelle
Dutch hollandais

E
each chaque
  each person/day/night par personne/
  jour/nuit
  each (one) chacun(e)
ear une oreille
early de bonne heure
to earn/win gagner
east l'est (m)
Easter Pâques (f.pl)
easy facile
to eat manger
economics l'économie (f)
to economise économiser
edge le bord
Edinburgh Edimbourg
education l'enseignement (m)/
  l'éducation (f)
effort un effort
  it's not worth the effort ce n'est pas...
  la peine
egg un oeuf
elbow le coude

eldest aîné(e)
electric électrique
electrician un électricien
electricity l'électricité (f)
elegant élégant(e)
e-mail l'électronique (f)
emergency une urgence
emergency exit la sortie de secours
employee un(e) employé(e)
employer un employeur
empty vide
end la fin/le bout
  at the end of au bout de
energy l'énergie (f)
engaged (number/seat/toilet)
  occupé(e)
  (of taxi) pris/pas libre
  (betrothed) fiancé(e)
engagement les fiançailles (f)
engine le moteur
England l'Angleterre (f)
English anglais(e)
to enjoy oneself s'amuser
enjoy your meal! bon appétit!
enough assez
  that's enough ça suffit!
to enrol s'inscrire
to enter entrer
entertainment la distraction
entirely entièrement/
  complètement/tout
  à fait/totalement
entrance une entrée
entrance fee le prix d'entrée
entry une entrée
  no entry défense d'entrer
envelope une enveloppe
epileptic épileptique
equal/the same égal(e)
equivalent value la contrevaleur
error une erreur
escalator un escalier roulant
espresso coffee un express
essential essentiel (-elle)
euro euro
Eurocheques des Eurochèques (m)
Europe l'Europe (f)
European européen(ne)
even même
evening le soir/la soirée

in the evening le soir/en soirée
  good evening! Bonsoir!
every tout/chaque
everybody tout le monde
everywhere partout
exact juste/exact(e)
exactly exactement
to exaggerate exagérer
example un example
to exceed excéder/dépasser
excellent excellent(e)
except (for) sauf/à part/à l'exception de
excess fare/excess charge
  le supplément
to exchange échanger/changer
exchange un échange
exchange bureau le bureau de change
exchange rate (at today's price)
  le cours du change (au cours du jour)
excursion une excursion
excuse me! Excusez-moi/pardon!
exhibition une exposition
to exist exister
exit la sortie
  emergency exit la sortie de secours
to expect compter
expenditure la dépense
expenses les frais (m)
expensive cher (chère)
  not very expensive pas très
  cher (chère)
to explain expliquer
expression/phrase une expression
extension (phone) le poste
extra en plus/supplémentaire
extraordinary extraordinaire
extremely extrêmement
eye un oeil (pl yeux)

F
face la figure/le visage
face flannel le gant de toilette
facing en face de/faisant face à
factory une usine
fair (hair) blond(e)
false faux (fausse)
family la famille
famous célèbre
far (from) loin (de)
  as far as jusqu'à

fare le prix du billet
  at normal fare à tarif normal
  at reduced fare à tarif réduit
  fare stage la section
farm la ferme
father le père
father-in-law le beau-père
February février
to feel (se) sentir
ferry le ferry
  by ferry en ferry
festival (musical) le festival
fiancé le fiancé/la fiancée
field le champ
to fight se battre
to fill (in) remplir
to fill up with petrol faire le plein
fillet le filet
film (for camera) la pellicule
  (in cinema) le film
to find trouver
fine (penalty) la contravention/
  une amende
fine (weather) beau (temps)
fine (OK) bien/d'accord
finger le doigt
to finish finir
fire! Au feu!
fireman le (sapeur-)pompier
first premier (-ère)
  first of all d'abord
fish le poisson
fishing la pêche
fitted out aménagé(e)
to fix fixer/arranger/réparer
fixed-price menu le menu à prix fixe
flash le flash
flat un appartement
flats (block of) un immeuble
flavour le parfum
flight le vol
floor (storey) un étage
floor (= boards) le plancher/le parquet
  ground floor le rez-de-chaussée
  on the floor par terre
flower la fleur
flu la grippe
fog/mist le brouillard/la brume
to follow suivre

food les provisions (f)
  sea food les fruits (m) de mer
food store une alimentation
foot le pied
  on foot à pied
football le football
footpath le sentier/le chemin
for pour
  for (= because) car
forbidden interdit/défendu
  it is forbidden to... défense de...
foreign étranger (-ère)
forest la forêt
to forget oublier
to forgive pardonner/excuser
  forgive me excusez-moi
fork la fourchette
form la fiche, le bon
  order form le bon de commande
formula le formulaire
France la France
free libre/gratuit
freezer le congélateur
French français(e)
Friday vendredi
fried potatoes pommes frites
friend un(e) ami(e)/un copain
  (une copine)
frightening effrayant
frontier la frontière
fruit le fruit
fruit juice le jus de fruit
fruiterer le marchand de fruits
frying pan la poêle
full (capacity) plein
full (= no vacancies) complet
  (complète)
full board la pension complète
fun fair la fête foraine
furnished meublé(e)
furnishing l'ameublement (m)
fuse le plomb/le fusible

G
game le jeu
games room la salle de jeux
gangster film un film de gangsters
garage le garage
garage mechanic le garagiste

garden le jardin
gas le gaz
gate/fence la barrière
gear la vitesse
general général
generally généralement/en général
gentle doux (-ce)
geography la géographie
German allemand(e)
Germany l'Allemagne (f)
to get on together s'entendre
gift le cadeau
to gift wrap faire un paquet-cadeau
gin le gin
girl la jeune fille
to give donner
 to give back rendre
glass le verre
 to raise one's glass (toast) lever
 son verre
glasses les lunettes (f)
glove le gant
to go aller
 to go and fetch/go for aller chercher
 to go and see aller voir
 to go around with fréquenter
 to go away s'en aller
 to go camping faire du camping
 to go down descendre
 to go home/back rentrer
 to go in entrer
 to go out sortir
 to go up monter
 to go with accompagner
goal le but
gold l'or
 made of gold en or
golf course le terrain de golf
good bon(ne)
 good (at a subject) fort(e)
goodbye au revoir
goodness! tiens!/mon Dieu!
gram le gramme
grandchild le petit-enfant (pl petits-enfants)
granddaughter la petite-fille
grandfather le grand-père
grandmother la grand-mère
grandparent le grand-parent
grandson le petit-fils

grape le raisin
grapefruit le pamplemousse
grass l'herbe (f)
Great Britain la Grande Bretagne
green vert(e)
Green Card la carte verte
greengrocer le marchand de légumes
grey gris(e)
grocer un épicier
grocer's une alimentation/une épicerie
ground le terrain
 on the ground par terre
ground floor le rez-de-chaussée
group le groupe
to guarantee garantir
 guarantee le bon de garantie
guide le guide
guilty coupable
gust le coup de vent
gym/PE la gym
 gym (PE room) la salle de gym
gymnastics la gymnastique

H

hair les cheveux (m)
hairdresser le coiffeur/la coiffeuse
half demi/la moitié
half-board la demi-pension
half-time la mi-temps
hall le vestibule
 town hall un hôtel de ville
ham le jambon
hand la main
handbag le sac à main
handkerchief le mouchoir
to hang up (phone) raccrocher
haricot beans les haricots (m)
hat le chapeau
to have avoir
to have to devoir
 I have to je dois
head la tête
headlight le phare
health la santé
 good health/cheers à la tienne/à
 la vôtre!
to hear entendre
heart le coeur
heart attack la crise cardiaque

heat la chaleur
heating le chauffage
heatwave la vague de chaleur
to heel (a shoe) remettre un talon à
hello! bonjour!
 (on the phone) allô!
to help secourir/aider
 help! au secours!
here ici
here is/here are voici
herring un hareng
hi! salut!
highway code le code de la route
hike/ramble la randonnée
to hire louer
hiring la location
to hitchhike faire de l'autostop
hobby le passe-temps/le hobby
hockey le hockey
hold the line! ne quittez pas!
hole le trou
holiday (vacation) les vacances (f)
Holland la Hollande/les Pays-Bas (m)
to hope espérer
horse le cheval
hospital un hôpital
hostess une hôtesse
 air hostess une hôtesse de l'air
hot chaud(e)
hotel un hôtel
hour une heure
house/home la maison/le domicile
 at my house chez moi
hovercraft un aéroglisseur
how comment
 how do I get to...? pour aller à...?
 how long? (time) combien de temps?
 how much? combien?
 how much is it? c'est combien?
hunger la faim
 I am hungry j'ai faim
hurt blessé(e)
husband le mari
hypermarket un hypermarché

I

ice/ice cream la glace
identification la pièce d'identité
identity une identité

if si
ill malade
illegal illégal
immediately immédiatement/tout de
 suite
important important(e)
impossible impossible
in dans/en
included compris(e)
indicator le clignotant
information les renseignements/
 le syndicat d'initiative
injection la piqûre
insect un insecte
inspector (train) le contrôleur
instead of au lieu de
insurance l'assurance (f)
insured assuré(e)
to intend avoir l'intention (de)
interesting intéressant(e)
international international(e)
interval un entracte
intolerable inadmissible
to introduce présenter
 may I introduce je te/vous présente
invitation une invitation
Ireland l'Irlande (f)
Nothern Ireland l'Irlande du Nord
Irish irlandais(e)
island une île
isn't it n'est-ce pas?
Italian italien (italienne)

J

jacket la veste/le blouson
jam la confiture
January janvier
jar le pot
jeans le jean
jersey le tricot
jobless au chômage
joiner/carpenter le menuisier
journalist le/la journaliste
journey le voyage
 have a good journey! bon voyage!
jug le pichet/la carafe
juice le jus
July juillet
jumper le tricot/le pull

June juin

K
to keep garder
key la clef
kilo le kilo
kind aimable
to kiss embrasser
kitchen la cuisine
knife le couteau
knob le bouton
to knock frapper
  to knock down/over renverser
to know (a fact) savoir
  to know (a person) connaître

L
ladder une échelle
lady la dame
lager la bière blonde
lake le lac
lamb un agneau
lamp la lampe
language la langue
large grand(e)
last dernier (-ère)
  at last enfin
late tard/en retard
later tout à l'heure/plus tard
launderette la laverie automatique
lavatory le WC/le cabinet de toilette
leaflet/folder le dépliant
leather le cuir
  made of leather en cuir
to leave quitter/partir
left gauche
  on the left à gauche
leg la jambe
leisure le loisir
  leisure-time activities les loisirs (m)
lemon le citron
lemon juice le jus de citron
lemonade la limonade
to lend prêter
length (of time) la durée
less moins
  a little less un peu moins
to let laisser
letter la lettre

letter box la boîte aux lettres
lettuce la salade
library la bibliothèque
licence la licence
  driving licence le permis de conduire
lift un ascenseur
lift pass le forfait
to lift the receiver décrocher le
  combiné
to light allumer
light (weight) léger (-ère)
light (colour) clair(e)
light la lumière/la lampe
  (car) le phare
  rear light le feu arrière
  red light le feu rouge
  side lights les feux de position
  traffic light le feu
  dipped headlights les feux de
    croisement
  headlights les feux de route
lighter le briquet
to like aimer
  I'd like je voudrais/j'aimerais
lilo le matelas pneumatique
line la ligne
list la liste
litre le litre
little petit(e)
  a little un peu
to live demeurer/habiter/vivre/résider
liver le foie
loaf le pain/la baguette
to loathe avoir horreur de
lobster le homard
to lock fermer à clef
London Londres
long long
  a long time longtemps
to look (at) regarder
  to look (for) chercher
lorry le camion
  heavy goods vehicle le poids lourd
to lose perdre
lost property office le bureau des
  objets trouvés
a lot beaucoup
  a lot (of) beaucoup (de)
love l'amour (m)

in love amoureux (-euse)
lovely beau (belle)/ravissant(e)
lozenge la pastille
luck la chance
  good luck! bonne chance!
left luggage locker la consigne
  automatique
luggage les bagages (m)
luggage rack le filet
lunch le déjeuner
  to have lunch déjeuner
luxury de luxe

M
machine la machine
  washing machine la machine à laver
Madam Madame
magazine le magazine/la revue
  weekly magazine un hebdomadaire
mail le courrier
to make faire
make-up le maquillage
man un homme
manager le directeur
map la carte
  road map la carte routière
March mars
market le marché
married marié(e)
to marry épouser/se marier avec
mashed (potatoes) pommes
  duchesse/pommes mousseline
match une allumette
  boxing match le match de boxe
  football match le match de football
material/fabric une étoffe
May mai
mayonnaise la mayonnaise
meal le repas
  cooked meal le plat cuisiné
  ready-cooked meal le repas préparé
  enjoy your meal! bon appétit!
meat la viande
mechanic le mécanicien/
  la mécanicienne
  garage mechanic/owner le garagiste
medicine la médecine/le médicament/le
  remède

Mediterranean Sea la Méditerranée
medium cooked (of meat) à point
meeting la conférence/la réunion/
  le rendezvous
  to arrange a meeting with prendre
  rendez-vous avec
melon le melon
member le/la membre
to mend raccommoder/réparer
menu la carte/le menu
metal le métal
  made of metal en métal/de métal
midday midi
middle le milieu
  in the middle (of) au milleu (de)
midnight minuit
milk le lait
million le million
mineral water l'eau minérale
minute la minute
to miss manquer
Miss Mademoiselle
mistake une erreur
mixture (medicine) le sirop
mobile phone le portable
modern moderne
moment un instant/un moment
Monday lundi
money l'argent (m)
  pocket money l'argent de poche
month le mois
monument le monument
moped la mobylette
more plus
  a little more un peu plus
morning le matin/la matinée
most of la plupart de
  at the most au plus
mother la mère
mother-in-law la belle-mère
motorbike la moto/le vélomoteur
  by motorbike à (en) moto/à (en)
  vélomoteur
motor-cyclist le motocycliste
motorway une autoroute
mountain la montagne
mouth la bouche
much beaucoup

how much? combien?
mum/mummy maman
municipal municipal(e)
museum le musée
mushroom le champignon
music la musique
 pop music la musique pop
musical musical(e)
mussels les moules (f)
mustard la moutarde

N

name le nom
 Christian/first name le prénom
narrow étroit(e)
nationality la nationalité
nationality plate la plaque de
 nationalité
near près de/proche
near here près d'ici
necessary nécessaire
 it is necessary il faut
neck le cou
necklace le collier
to need avoir besoin de
 I need j'ai besoin de
needle une aiguille
nephew le neveu
net (price) net (nette)
 net (for fish) le filet
never jamais
new nouveau (nouvelle)/neuf (neuve)
news les informations (f)/les actualités (f)
newspaper le journal
next (in order) prochain(e)
 next (to) à côté (de)
nice gentil (-ille)
niece la nièce
night la nuit
 goodnight! bonne nuit!
nil zéro
no non/pas (de)
noise le bruit
noodles les nouilles (f)
noon midi
Normandy la Normandie
north le nord
North Sea la Mer du Nord

nose le nez
not pas (de)/ne...pas
not at all pas du tout
note le billet (de dix euros, etc).
nothing rien
to notice remarquer
November novembre
number le numéro
nurse un infirmier/une infirmière
nylon le nylon
 made of nylon en nylon

O

occupied occupé(e)
October octobre
offence (against the law) une infraction
office le bureau
 foreign exchange office le bureau de
 change
 lost property office le bureau des
 objets trouvés
 ticket office le guichet
officer (policeman) Monsieur l'agent
OK d'accord/entendu
 it's OK ça va
 are you OK? ça va?/ça colle?
old ancien (-enne)/vieux (vieille)
omelette une omelette
on sur
one-way sens unique
onion un oignon
open ouvert(e)
 open on Mondays ouvert le lundi
opera un opéra
operation une opération
operator le/la téléphoniste
 international operator le service
 international
opposite en face de/ci-contre
optician un opticien
or ou
orange une orange
 orange juice le jus d'orange
 orangeade une orangeade/une
 orangina
orchestra un orchestre
to order commander
original original(e)

in the original language en version
originale
overcoat le pardessus
overcooked trop cuit(e)
to overtake dépasser
owner le propriétaire
  owner (of café) le patron
oysters les huîtres (f)

P

packet le paquet
pain la douleur
  to have a pain (in) avoir mal (à)
pair la paire
pal le copain (la copine)
pale pâle
pamphlet la brochure
pancake la crêpe
panties le slip
paper le papier
  writing paper le papier à lettres
  newspaper/magazine le journal
papers les papiers (m)
parcel le colis/le paquet
parent le parent
park le parc/le jardin public
  car park le parking/le stationnement
to park stationner/(se) garer
part la pièce
  spare part la pièce de rechange
part-time à temps partiel
party la surprise-partie/la boum
to pass/spend (time) passer
passenger le passager
passer-by le passant
passport le passeport
pasta les pâtes (f)
pastille/lozenge la pastille
pastry (cake) la pâtisserie
pâté le pâté
path le chemin/le sentier
pavement le trottoir
to pay payer
  to pay back rembourser
paying (not free) payant
payment le règlement/le paiement
peach la pêche
pear la poire

peas les pois (m)
  garden peas les petits pois
pedestrian le piéton
  pedestrian crossing le passage clouté
pencil le crayon
penfriend le/la correspondant(e)
penicillin la pénicilline
people les gens (m)
  a lot of people beaucoup de monde
pepper le poivre
peppery/spicy piquant(e)
per par
per day/person/night par jour/
personne/nuit
perfect parfait(e)
performance la séance
perfume le parfum
perfumery la parfumerie
period pains les règles (f) douloureuses
permanent permanent(e)
permission la permission
person la personne
  per person par personne
personal personnel (-elle)
petrol l'essence
  2/3-star/standard l'ordinaire (m)
  4/5-star/top-grade le super
petrol attendant le/la pompiste
petrol station la station-service
to phone téléphoner
photo la photo
physics la physique
piano le piano
picnic le pique-nique
piece le morceau
pig le cochon
pill la pilule
pillow un oreiller
pilot le pilote
pineapple un ananas
pitch/ground le terrain
place un endroit/un lieu
  to take place avoir lieu
plaice le cabillaud
to plan organiser
plan le plan
plane un avion
  by plane en avion/par avion

plant la plante
plaster le sparadrap
plastic le plastique
  made of plastic en plastique/
  de plastique
plate une assiette
platform le quai/la voie
to play jouer
  to play football jouer au football
  to play music jouer de la musique
  to play the piano jouer du piano
play la pièce de théâtre
pleasant agréable
please s'il te (vous) plaît
pleased content(e)
plug (electricity) la prise (de courant)
  plug (water) le tampon
plum la prune
plumber le plombier
pocket la poche
to point out indiquer
police la police/la gendarmerie
police station le commissariat/le poste
  de police/la gendarmerie
police van le car de police
policeman un agent de police/
  un gendarme
policewoman la femme-agent de police
policy (life insurance) la police
  d'assurance
pop (music) le pop
pork le porc
pork products la charcuterie
port le port
porter le porteur
possible possible
  is it possible? est-ce possible?
to post mettre à la poste/poster
post la poste/le courrier
post office le bureau de poste/les
  PTT/les P et T
postal order le mandat postal
postbox la boîte aux lettres
postcard la carte postale
postcode le code postal
poster/notice une affiche
postman le facteur
potato la pomme de terre

poultry la volaille
pound la livre
pound sterling la livre sterling
prawns les crevettes (roses) (f)/les
  langoustines (f)
to prefer préférer/aimer mieux
prescription une ordonnance
present le cadeau
pretty joli(e)
price le prix
  maximum price le prix maximum
  minimum price le prix minimum
price list le tarif
priority (to vehicles on the right)
  priorité à droite
  (over secondary road users) passage
  protégé
  to have priority avoir la priorité/avoir
  le droit (de passage)
private privé(e)
private hospital la clinique
profession le métier/la profession
programme le progamme
  programme (on TV) une émission
Protestant protestant(e)
pudding le dessert
to pull tirer
pullover le pull(over)
punctured crevée(e)
purchase un achat
purse le porte-monnaie
to put mettre/poser
pyjamas un pyjama
Pyrenees les Pyrénées (f)

Q
quantity la quantité
quay le quai
queen la reine
question la question
quickly vite/rapidement
  too quickly trop vite
quiet calme

R
rabbit le lapin
racing
  horse racing les courses (f) de

chevaux
  motor racing les courses (f) d'auto
radiator le radiateur
radio la radio
railway le chemin de fer
  French Railway la SNCF
to rain pleuvoir
  it's raining il pleut
raincoat un imperméable
rare rare
rare (of meat) saignant(e)
raspberry la framboise
rate (of exchange) le taux de change
  reduced rate tarif réduit
razor le rasoir
to read lire
ready prêt(e)
rear l'arrière (m)
rear-view mirror le rétroviseur
receipt le reçu
receiver le combiné
  to lift the receiver décrocher le
  combiné
reception office le bureau d'accueil
receptionist la réceptionniste
to recommend recommander/
  conseiller
record le disque
record player le tourne-disque/la
  platine
recreation la distraction
rectangular rectangulaire
red rouge
reduction la réduction
to refuse refuser
region la région
registration certificate la carte
  d'immatriculation
registration number le numéro
  d'immatriculation
registration plate la plaque
  d'immatriculation
to regret/be sorry regretter
regulations le règlement
to remain rester/demeurer
to rent/hire louer
  rent le loyer

renting/hiring la location
to repair réparer
  repair la réparation
  repair kit la trousse de réparation
to repeat répéter
  will you repeat that voulez-vous
  répéter ça?
reply la réponse
report (on an accident) le constat
reservation la réservation
to reserve réserver
to rest se reposer
rest (remainder) le reste
restaurant le restaurant
to return retourner
return (ticket) un aller-retour
Rhine le Rhin
rib la côte
rice le riz
ride la randonnée
right
  to have a right avoir le droit
  you are right vous avez raison
  on the right à droite
  just right à point
  (= not wrong) correct(e)/juste
to ring sonner
ring un anneau/une bague
ripe mûr(e)
  nicely ripe à point
road la route/le chemin
  trunk road la route nationale/la
  grande route
roadway la chaussée
roadworks les travaux (m)
roast rôti(e)
roll le petit pain
romance (film/book) un film/livre
  d'amour
roof le toit
room la pièce/la salle
  waiting room la salle d'attente
rope la corde
round (adj) rond(e)
  (around) autour (de)
  all around tout autour
route un itinéraire

bus route la ligne d'autobus
rowing boat la barque
rucksack le sac à dos
rugby le rugby
rules le règlement
to run courir
  to run over renverser/écraser
Russia la Russie
Russian russe

S

safety belt la ceinture de sécurité
sailboard la planche à voile
salad(s) les crudités (f)/la salade
salami le saucisson
sales les soldes (f)
  in a sale en solde
salesman/woman le vendeur/
  la vendeuse
salmon le saumon
salt le sel
salty salé(e)
same même/pareil(le)
sand le sable
sandal la sandale
sandwich le sandwich
sardine la sardine
satisfied satisfait(e)
Saturday samedi
saucer la soucoupe
sauerkraut la choucroûte
sausage le saucisson
to say dire
scampi les langoustines (f) frites
scene la vue
school une école
scooter (motor) le scooter
Scotland l'Ecosse (f)
Scottish écossais(e)
screen un écran
screwdriver le tournevis
sea la mer
seafood les fruits (m) de mer
seasickness le mal de mer
  I am seasick j'ai le mal de mer
seat le siège
seated assis(e)

second deuxième
second-class ticket une seconde
to see voir
  see you! à tout à l'heure
self-service store/restaurant
  le libre-service
to sell vendre
to send envoyer
separately à part/séparément
September septembre
serious grave/sérieux
to serve servir
service (not) included service
  (non) compris
to set off partir
several plusieurs
sex le sexe
to feel shaky se sentir fragile
shampoo le shampooing
sharp pointu(e)
sheep le mouton
sheet (bed) le drap
  sheet (paper) la feuille
shirt la chemise
shivers des frissons (m)
shoe la chaussure
shoe repairer's la cordonnerie
to shop/go shopping faire les courses
  shop la boutique/le magasin
short court(e)
shorts le short
to show montrer
show le spectacle
  film show la séance de cinéma
shower la douche
  to have a shower prendre une douche
shower block le bloc sanitaire
shrimps les crevettes grises
shutter le volet
sick malade
side le côte
to sign signer
silk la soie
  made of silk en soie
silver l'argent (m)
  made of silver en argent
since depuis

singer le chanteur/la chanteuse
single (ticket) un aller simple
sink un évier/un bac à vaisselle
sister la sœur
sit down! asseyez-vous!
size/waist la taille
size (for shoes/gloves) la pointure
skates les patins (m)
skating rink la patinoire
ski/skiing le ski
 ski boots les chaussures (f) de ski
 ski equipment un équipement de ski
 skiing lesson la leçon de ski
 ski instructor le moniteur/la monitrice
 ski jumping le saut à skis
 ski lift le téléski/le télésiège
 ski pants le fuseau
 ski resort la station de ski
 ski slopes les pentes de ski
 ski sticks les bâtons de ski
 ski-touring le ski de randonnée
 ski tow le téléski
skirt la jupe
sledge la luge
to sleep dormir
sleeping bag le sac de couchage
slice la tranche
slim/slight mince
slot la fente
to slow down ralentir
slowly lentement
small petit(e)
smart chic
smell une odeur
to smoke fumer
 (no-) smoking (non-) fumeur
snack bar le snack
soap le savon
society la société
sock la chaussette
socket la prise (de courant)
sole (fish) la sole
 (on shoe) la semelle
 to sole a shoe ressemeler un soulier
son le fils
song la chanson
soon bientôt

see you soon! à bientôt!
sorry! pardon!/excusez-moi!
 I'm sorry je m'excuse/je suis désolé(e)
Sound and Light (spectacle) Son et
 Lumière
soup le potage/la soupe
south le sud
souvenir le souvenir
Spain l'Espagne (m)
Spanish espagnol(e)
spare parts les pièces de rechange
to speak parler
speciality la spécialité
spectacles les lunettes (f)
speed la vitesse
 speed limit la limitation de vitesse
to spell épeler
to spend (time) passer
 to spend (money) dépenser
spicy piquant(e)
spinach les épinards (m)
spoon la cuillère
 coffee spoon la cuiller à café
 spoonful la cuillerée
sport le sport
 sports facilities les équipements (m)
 sportifs
 winter sports les sports d'hiver
spouse un époux/une épouse
to sprain (one's ankle) se fouler (la
 cheville)
spring le printemps
 in spring au printemps
square la place
square (adj) carré(e)
stadium le stade
staircase un escalier
stalls le parterre/l'orchestre (m)
stamp le timbre
 a one-euro stamp un timbre à un euro
star (of film) la vedette
to start commencer
 to start (car engine) démarrer
station la gare
station (Metro) la station
to stay rester
 stay le séjour

steak le steak/le biftek
steak and chips steak-frites
to steal voler
steam la vapeur
steering wheel le volant
stepfather le beau-père
stick le bâton
  French stick (thick) la baguette
  (thin) la ficelle
to sting piquer
stockings les bas
stomach le ventre/l'estomac (m)
to stop arrêter/s'arrêter
store le dépôt
stove le poêle
  oil (paraffin) stove le poêle à mazout
  (à pétrole)
strawberry la fraise
street la rue
string la ficelle
strong fort(e)
student un(e) étudiant(e)
sub-title le sous-titre
suburbs la banlieue
sugar le sucre
suitcase la valise
summer l'été (m)
  in summer en été
sun le soleil
sunburn un coup de soleil
Sunday dimanche
sunstroke une insolation/un coup de
  soleil
supermarket le supermarché
supplement le supplément
supplementary supplémentaire
sure sûr(e)
surf board la planche de surf
sweater le tricot/le pull
sweet le bonbon
sweet doux (douce)
sweet (=sweetened) sucré(e)
sweet shop la confiserie
sweetcorn le maïs
to swim nager
  swimming la natation
swimming pool (heated) la piscine
  chauffée

swimming pool (indoor) la piscine
  couverte
swimming pool (outdoor) la piscine en
  plein air
swimming trunks le maillot de bain
swimsuit le maillot de bain
Swiss suisse
switch un interrupteur
Switzerland la Suisse
syrup/mixture le sirop
  cough mixture le sirop contre la toux

T
table la table
tablet/pill le cachet/le comprimé
to take prendre
take-away à emporter
taken (of seat) occupé(e)
tap le robinet/la prise d'eau
tart la tarte
taxi le taxi
  by taxi en taxi
taxi rank le station de taxis
tea le thé
teenager un(e) adolescent(e)
tee-shirt le tee-shirt
to telephone téléphoner
  telephone le téléphone
  telephone box la cabine
  telephone call le coup de téléphone/
    le coup de fil
  telephone directory un annuaire
television la télévision/la télé
telex le télex
to tell dire
temperature la température
  I have a temperature j'ai de la
    température/de la fièvre
ten dix
tennis le tennis
  to play tennis jouer au tennis
  table tennis le tennis de table
  tennis courts les courts (m) de tennis
tent la tente
to thank remercier
thank you very much merci bien/
  beaucoup
that ça/cela

that's (of price total) ça fait
that way par là
theatre le théâtre
there y/là
there is/there are il y a/voilà
thief le voleur
third troisième
thirst la soif
I am thirsty j'ai soif
this ceci
thousand mille
thread le fil
throat la gorge
I have a sore throat j'ai mal à la gorge
Thursday jeudi
ticket le billet
ticket collector (at railway station)
le contrôleur
ticket office le guichet
tie la cravate
tights le collant
time le temps, la fois
on time à temps/à l'heure
a long time longtemps
at what time? à quelle heure?
tin (of food) la boîte
tin opener un ouvre-boîte
tip le pourboire
tired fatigué(e)
tobacco le tabac
tobacconist's le bureau de tabac/
le café/le tabac
today aujourd'hui
today's special le plat du jour
together ensemble
toilet la toilette/le cabinet/le WC
token le jeton
toll (gate) le péage
tomato la tomate
tomorrow demain
tongue la langue
too (much) trop
tool un outil
tooth la dent
toothache le mal de dents
toothbrush la brosse à dents
toothpaste le dentifrice/la pâte
dentifrice
to clean one's teeth se brosser

les dents
torch la lampe électrique
torn déchiré(e)
total le montant/le total/la somme
towel la serviette
hand towel un essuie-mains
tea towel le torchon
town la ville
toy le jouet
track/platform la voie
traffic light le feu
tragedy la tragédie
trailer (car) la remorque
trailer (cinema) la bande-annonce
trailer (tent) la tente remorque
train le train
express train un rapide
fast train un express
high-speed train un TGV
non-stop or through train un train
direct
stopping train un omnibus
by train par le train/en train
transfer un virement
to make a credit transfer faire un
virement
tray le plateau
tree un arbre
trip une excursion
trousers le pantalon
trout la truite
true vrai(e)
to try essayer
tube (of pills) le tube
tube (the Underground) le Métro
to go by the tube prendre le Métro
Tuesday mardi
tuna le thon
turkey la dinde
to turn tourner
TV la télé
TV news le télé-journal
twice deux fois
twin un jumeau/une jumelle
to twist tordre
two deux
table for two table à deux
tyre le pneu
burst tyre le pneu crevé

spare tyre le pneu de rechange

U

umbrella le parapluie
uncle un oncle
under sous
underdone saignant(e)
Underground le Métro
  by Underground en Métro
underpants le slip
to understand comprendre
underwear les sous-vêtements (m)
undrinkable (of water) non potable
United Kingdom le Royaume-Uni
university une université
unwell souffrant(e)
urgent urgent(e)
USA les Etats-Unis (m)
usherette une ouvreuse
useless inutile
usually généralement

V

vanilla la vanille
veal le veau
vegetable le légume
vehicle la voiture/le véhicule
very très
village le village
to visit visiter
  visitor le visiteur/la visiteuse
to vomit vomir

W

waist la taille
to wait (for) attendre
waiter le garçon (de café)/le serveur
waiting room la salle d'attente
waitress la serveuse
Wales le Pays de Galles
to walk marcher
  to go for a walk faire une promenade
  walk la promenade/la randonnée
wallet le portefeuille
to want vouloir
warden le guardien
wardrobe une armoire
warning un avertissement

warning sign un panneau avertisseur
to wash (se) laver
  to wash up faire la vaisselle
  wash (e.g. car wash) le lavage
washbasin le lavabo
washroom les toilettes (f)
wasp la guêpe
watch la montre
water l'eau (f)
water supply point la prise d'eau
to wear/carry porter
weather le temps
Wednesday mercredi
week la semaine
weekend le weekend
to weigh peser
well bien
Welsh gallois(e)
west l'ouest (m)
western (film) le western
wet mouillé(e)
what quoi/qu'est-ce que
wheel la roue
  spare wheel la roue de secours
  steering wheel le volant
when quand
where où
which quel(le)
whisky le whisky
white blanc (blanche)
Whitsuntide/Whit Sunday Pentecôte (f)
who qui
who's speaking? c'est de la part
  de qui?
whose/of which dont
why pourquoi
wide large
wife/woman la femme
to win gagner
window la fenêtre
  shop window la vitrine
windscreen le pare-brise
windscreen wiper un essuie-glace
wine le vin (blanc, rouge, rosé, etc.)
winter l'hiver (m)
winter sports les sports d'hiver
to wish/want vouloir
with avec

without sans
woman la femme
wood le bois/la forêt
  made of wood en bois
wool la laine
  made of wool en laine
to work travailler
  (= to be in working order) marcher
  it's not working ça ne marche pas
worn/worn out usé(e)
to write écrire
writing paper le papier à lettres
wrong faux (fausse)

to be wrong avoir tort

y
year un an/une année
yellow jaune
yesterday hier
yoghurt le yaourt
young jeune
youngest child le cadet/la cadette
youth hostel une auberge de jeunesse

Z
zero zéro

When you get back from your trip, try these **teach yourself** titles, available from all good bookshops and on-line retailers:

- **Teach Yourself One-Day French**, by Elisabeth Smith
  Only 50 words and phrases to learn with a 75-minute audio CD and an 8-page booklet. Join Andy and Lis on their flight to France and listen in to the 'One-Day French Challenge'!

- **Teach Yourself French Starter Kit**, by Elisabeth Smith
  Your personal tutor on two 70-minute CDs guides you through a 7-week programme. The coursebook, traveller's companion and flashcards make it easy.

- **Teach Yourself Instant French**, by Elisabeth Smith
  Learn French in 6 weeks, on a daily diet of 35 minutes. There's a book with audio support on CD or cassette.

Thinking of buying a property in France? You'll need

- **Teach Yourself Buying a Home in France**, by Peter MacBride with Monique Perceau
  The book will help you choose and buy a property abroad, and then will give you the words you'll need to help you restore or maintain it. 90 clearly labelled diagrams and help with the pronunciation on the essential language CD. (Available February 2005.)